Based on

25 Years of

Science, Psychology & Experience

Dedicated to

All those who suffer from Addiction

turning their 'Shoulds' into 'Musts'
One Day at a Time

and those that have lost
loved ones to Gambling

First Edition

published 12th February 2019
updated 26.02.19

Further information at:

GamblingAddiction.blog

GamHelp.org

INDEX

FIVE WAYS TO REPAIR AND UPGRADE YOUR MIND

NEW BEGINNINGS

APPENDICES

Introduction

Only people that have lived through addiction really understand it.

I myself have experienced the darkness, the complete compulsiveness of gambling, and paid the price. But since then I have built a life afterwards and managed to get a least some of my sanity back.

Why do I use the word 'sanity'? I think it was Einstein who famously said (and I paraphrase)

> *"Doing the same thing over and over again*
> *but expecting a different result*
> *is the definition of **Insanity**."*

That was me, and as you're reading this, more than likely you as well (or someone close to you).

And as any self-respecting Addict knows, you go from hit to hit, session to session, just to get through day. But this existence is far from actually *Living*. And before you realise it your life is very different from what it could have been, *should* have been.

But you know this already. Let's face it, nobody is going to pick up a book about Gambling Addiction unless they've been touched by it. You know first-hand what it's like to be a hamster in a wheel, going round and around, running but going nowhere.

Gambling isn't like in the movies where the handsome hero bets all with a glint in his eye, wins, then leaves with the person of their dreams while the crowd looks on enviously. It's the complete opposite of this. The Problem Gambler has usually already lost this months' wages (perhaps even next month's as well) and told so many lies that they can hardly keep track. Desperately chasing money in a cold sweat, their stress levels are through the roof. They are numb from the lies, adrenaline and the guilt, avoiding letters and calls from debt collectors, and exhausted by the effort of working all hours just to feed their habit. A happy, content life and a good night's sleep is a distant memory. In fact they often think their life is over.

WHY Gambling is Ruining your Life

Over the years I've known and been fortunate to have been able to help a lot of gamblers, most of them intelligent people with good jobs. Nearly all of them have asked *WHY* they gamble to extremes when others seem to be able to control it. But I was told early on in my own recovery that there is no point in looking for a reason, as it won't help you recover.

However that has always worried me slightly as the law of **Cause & Effect** is universal. Understanding *WHY* something occurs always has something to teach us about

HOW to best treat it, fix it, and ensure it doesn't happen again.

So I decided to write a book that would help people understand and address their gambling problem, as well as get to the bottom of *WHY* we gamble to excess.

Helping people get over their gambling problem was very familiar territory for me as I have been doing it every week for a quarter of a century.

But my research into WHY we gamble and the aspects of brain development and malfunction in Problem Gamblers was fresh information for me. Personally I am stunned by the findings. While the research is and has been openly available since the mid-nineties, it is not common knowledge. In my 35 years being around Gambling Addiction I had never come across it. Neither have most doctors and health professionals.

What We'll be Covering

Hopefully the information you find here will help answer many of the questions you have about your current behaviour, explain your past, and influence your future choices.

Best of all it shows you how to break free from this nightmare like I did, and stay free.

- Diagnosis – Quickly confirm whether you have a problem or not

- Behaviour - Learn what's different about your brain that makes you gamble compulsively from others that *can* stop

- Programmes - Five daily programs to kickstart your recovery and keep you on track

- Techniques – Five tried & tested ways to reprogram your brain and overcome your addiction

- Withdrawal - Learn how to minimise urges by hacking your mind

- Diet - Find out what foods help reduce urges (and help you stay off gambling)

- Exercise - Discover which types of exercise helps you quit the fastest

- Mistakes - Find out the common ways people slip up and how to avoid them

- Support - Find out where to get free daily support with your addiction

- Families - Understand how you can help your gambler recover

- Guidance - Practical tips on debt and money management

You'll also learn:

- About an *undiagnosed medical condition* that you may have, which explains why a key part of your brain is smaller than it should be and why you gamble differently to most people

- How, once you start gambling, that same part of your brain actually *shuts down* making you unable to stop or even walk away until you have run out of money

- About cases where a million addicts to one of the hardest drugs there is experienced *spontaneous remission*, and what was present that made this happen

This is a book for *everyone* touched by gambling – problem gamblers that need help, gamblers that are already getting help through GA or a therapist, and the friends & family that have questions. It's a condensed mixture of Science, Experience and Wisdom gathered over 25 years of having lived it. You will all find something that you can use.

Either read the whole thing cover to cover, and use it as a guide to get your sanity and your life back on track rapidly. Or dip in and out of it like a Reference Manual, using the bits you need right now.

But trust me, you should read all of it as every chapter contains something useful that you probably are not aware of yet.

Will Reading this Book Help?

Even if you just read the book cover to cover and implement none of it, you will at least know the truth about what you do and why you do it.

But I GUARANTEE that anyone who follows the guidance here and implements it daily for a period of time will make a full and speedy recovery. These strategies and methods are already in use by over hundreds of thousands of addicts worldwide, and they work. You WILL get your life back - just do what has worked for others.

The biggest battle you will face is your own gambling-wired mind, that inner voice of doubt and laziness that constantly niggles: *"Do I really need to do that?"* And then the: *"I haven't gambled for two weeks - surely I must be cured by now?"* voice. That kind of self-talk keeps us prisoner to the addiction, and I've included some daily practices that will help with that too.

So if you're physically and mentally *sick* of what gambling has done to you, and prepared to do whatever it takes to get your sanity back, then let's get started.

Mike
25 years gambling free

BE PART OF THE SOLUTION!

I don't know about you, but I am appalled by the lack of help and support for vulnerable Gambling Addicts and their families.

I am determined to address this, and at the back of this book you will find a list of the projects I am currently working on.

If you feel this book helps you or your family in any way, I would be most grateful of your donations at **CrowdfundMe.co.uk** to help get these lifesaving projects underway. We are totally independent and not for profit - every little helps.

Thank You

CHASING RAINBOWS

Chapter I
What IS Gambling Addiction?

A Gambling Addict is best summed up as someone who is no longer able to regulate their gambling. They spend more *Time* than they intended, and more *Money* than they planned, pretty much every time.

Gambling ends up causing problems in many areas of such a person's life – Financial, Family, Relationships, Career, and Health.

At its core, gambling addiction is putting **short term pleasure** ahead of **long term misery**.

But it's best summed up by the people that have experienced it:

"It's like being a rat in wheel going round and around."

"I didn't realise it at the time, but I put Gambling above everyone and everything else in my life."

"I would start out with good intentions, but within hours it had all gone to SH*T."

"I borrowed from friends, from family, stole from my employer – all because of my gambling."

"I told people what they wanted to hear as I knew they couldn't handle the truth."

"I would be up then down, like on some kind of emotional rollercoaster."

I was existing from day to day, bet to bet… I wouldn't call it living."

"It's like I took a wrong turn somewhere and my life turned out different to how it should have."

"The only time I feel at peace is when all the money's gone and I can't do it anymore."

"I exceeded every limit I ever set myself, every time."

Quick Facts

Some 63% of adults have gambled in the past year, research from the UK Gambling Commission suggests.

It found little difference between the sexes - 66% of all men and 59% of all women took part in some form of gambling, including the lottery.

But men were x7.5 times more likely than women to become a Problem Gambler - which the Gambling Commission defines as *someone whose habit compromises, disrupts or damages family, personal or recreational pursuits.*

- Around 1% of the 66m UK population have a problem with gambling, between 430,000 – 2,000,000 Problem Gamblers (according to the Gambling Commission)

- 55,000 Children under 16 develop a gambling problem through gaming and many go on to mainstream gambling sites using their parents' card details

- Up to 2 people a day commit gambling-related suicide, as they see no other escape from their pain

- Untreated gambling addiction contributes hugely to rising divorce rates, bankruptcy, imprisonment, and homelessness

- Gambling is now the second biggest factor behind UK Employee Fraud (up SIX times on last year)

- Gambling costs the NHS £1.2Billion a year in associated costs:
  - hospital inpatient services (£140m–£610m)
  - mental health primary care (£10m–£40m)
  - secondary mental health services (£30m–£110m)

- There is only *one* NHS Problem Gambling Clinic in the UK

- **450,000 problem gamblers**, but approximately 95% of them are still suffering:

Gamblers Anonymous	8,000
GamCare	8,000
NHS	1,000
Independent Counsellors/Therapists	1,000
Total Getting Help	**18,000**

Chapter 2
Am I a Compulsive Gambler?

First things first, what exactly IS a *Compulsive* Gambler? Otherwise known as a Problem Gambler, Pathological or Abnormal Gambler.

Perhaps the easiest definition of a Problem Gambler is someone for whom gambling causes problems in their life. And they try to gamble their way out. Gambling is the only addiction where *One More* is seen as the solution – not just "one more and then I'll quit" but "one more and then I *will be able* quit."

This is someone who has a Compulsion, an uncontrollable desire, a *Need* to Gamble. A need so strong that it feels like their brain is physically twitching, and when it starts they have tunnel vision and can't think of anything else. A person that is extreme, often up then very down, like they will go crazy if they don't get their gambling fix.

Or as addiction expert Dr Gabor Matè puts it:

"Addiction is a complex psychological & physiological process which manifests itself in ANY behaviour that a person enjoys, finds relief in, and craves in the short term but suffers negative consequences in the long term, and doesn't give up despite the negative consequences."

So there you have it:

> 1. Craving pleasure/relief in short term
> 2. Consequences in long term
> 3. Inability to give it up

However if you *are* able to gamble but don't lose more than you can afford and often walk away with money, don't lose sleep and don't have to lie to cover up your gambling, then you're most probably NOT a problem or compulsive Gambler.

But if you are HONEST with yourself and answer YES to more than 5 of the following questions, then this book is definitely for you:

1. Would your partner, friends or family say you have a gambling problem?
2. Have you ever tried to stop or control your gambling?
3. Do you gamble longer than you planned?
4. Do you often gamble until your cash is gone or cards / accounts are empty?
5. Do you lose time from work due to gambling?
6. Is gambling making your home life unhappy?
7. Has gambling ever cost you a job or other opportunity?

8. Is gambling causing a decrease in your ambition or efficiency?
9. Have you ever felt guilty after gambling?
10. Do you wake up in the morning and feel an urge to return to gambling?
11. Have you ever taken out loans after you've gambled your own money?
12. Does gambling cause you to have difficulty in sleeping?
13. Do you ever gamble to escape worry or trouble?
14. Do you feel the need to celebrate or reward yourself with a bit of gambling?
15. Do arguments, disappointments, or frustration create an urge to gamble?
16. Does your gambling make you careless of the welfare of your family?
17. Have you ever sold anything to finance your gambling?
18. Do you need more gambling & bigger bets to get the same excitement?
19. Do you lie to cover up your gambling?
20. Have you ever considered killing yourself as a result of your gambling?

How did you do?

- **1-4 Points**: A person without a problem / addiction will typically score **4 or less,** but there are still signs of a problem beginning that you need addressing before it gets worse

- **5-12 Points**: A person with a compulsion will say YES to **at least 5** of the questions

- **13-20 Points**: A person is who is no longer in control of their gambling activity will answer YES to **13 questions or more**, and certainly <u>YES</u> to:

  [Qu.2]: *have you ever tried to stop before, and*
  [Qu.19]: *lying to keep your gambling secret*

* * *

SUMMARY

When we're gambling it's all about the Money. What we've lost, how we're going to replace it or win it back, and what excuses we're going to have to make in order to cover up that we gambled it away.

But as your answers to these questions might suggest, there is a lot more to your Gambling Addiction than you think. Most of the problem gamblers I have ever met answer YES to at least 16 out of 20, and unless they admit their problem, soon make 20/20.

EXERCISE

Write **your story**, your journey so far with relation to Gambling.

Start with your first gambling experiences right up to present day. This is a short story or *"Therapy"* as they call it in GA, and is your first step in coming to terms with your problem.

It can take you 5 minutes or 5 hours, it's up to you. But make sure you include your main gambling experiences and the consequences and your feelings. Not just about what's gambling done to you, but what it's done to the people close to you. Keep this as you're going to need to refer to it later.

Do it *now* please before proceeding, it will help you get the most from this book. Do it even if you haven't bet for some time.

And if you're having a problem writing it, what's the worst that can happen? No-one's going to see it but you. You didn't pick up this book to do nothing - stop making excuses and get on with it!

Chapter 3
The Dreamworld of the Problem Gambler

A common characteristic of the Abnormal Gambler is the Dreamworld they escape into, sometimes described as a their 'Bubble'.

They might escape to this Dreamworld:

PHYSICALLY:

- in a Bookies
- in a Casino
- in an Arcade, Bingo or Snooker hall
- some other establishment

where they settle themselves in for a short time... which invariably turns into a long time.

VIRTUALLY:

With the huge rise of online gambling on mobile devices, gamblers can now escape to their dreamworld at work, in their car, at home, or anywhere they can get WIFI or adequate reception.

It is entirely common for someone to be gambling 3 feet from you, in a meeting or in the living room, but as you can't directly see their phone or laptop screen you are completely unaware.

Online Gamblers have become increasingly sophisticated at covering their tracks, by having multiple betting sites open in hidden tabs while their work remains visible on screen, waiting for a 30 second window when they can discretely check scores or place another bet. Or hop off to the rest room for yet another (gambling) break. IBS has got a lot to answer for.

With smart phones, we have any form of gambling you can imagine right in our pockets, 24/7.

People are more likely to become addicted to anything that has the 3 'A's :

Accessibility, **A**ffordability, **A**nonymity.

While in action the Gambler enters their fantasy world, where they might think any number of the following:

- *Today is going to be different..*
- *This time I'm going to stick to my limits..*
- *It's going to come in this time..*
- *When I win I'm going take everyone on holiday!*
- *It's due to payout soon, just got to ride it out..*
- *My luck's got to change soon..*
- *I've won – this time I can walk away, pay all my debts and never come back!!*

All these might come true for a *normal* Gambler, but sadly cannot be true for a gambling addict.

If they lose, they must chase their losses - even if it means spending £500 to chase £100, or £5000 to chase £500.

And if they win, they cannot walk away - and if by some miracle they do, it's only for a day or so. They are only at peace when all the money is gone (until next payday).

Staying in the Game

Why *can't* they walk away? We'll get into the biological reasons later on, but for now let's just say that the Gambler does not gamble to win.

*** EXCUSE ME? ***

Yes that's correct. You see a 'normal' Gambler - someone who does <u>not</u> gamble until their last pound is gone, someone who does <u>not</u> lie or feel guilty after gambling, and someone whose life is unaffected by gambling - CAN walk away.

In fact when they are up, they *enjoy* walking away, happy to hold on to their money or spend it wisely on something they want or need.

But to a *Problem* Gambler on the other hand, money is no longer money. It's Chips, Credits, Spins, Free Bets, Tickets - anything but actual money.

And when in action the Gambler is not thinking that they are playing with Money with which to buy food, pay the rent or mortgage, or go on holiday. They are totally immersed in the game they are playing and feel totally at home. In fact many Gamblers say that the only place they feel themselves is when they are gambling. You'll find out why this is physiologically the case later on.

So when we look at it in that context, a Win simply means we can gamble longer. More Credits, Chips, Spins or Bets. More playtime - more ME time.

And a loss means we have to go back to the cashpoint or use another card in order to keep gambling, until we run out.

What am I trying to Avoid or Escape from?

Do you remember Question 13 of the 20 Questions:

> *"Do you ever worry to escape worry or trouble?"*

Well this is question is often at the heart of problem gambling. We don't just gamble, we *use* gambling in a very specific way, and choose Fantasy over Reality in order to achieve it.

**Addiction isn't the primary problem
- it is an attempt to *solve* a problem.**

People give many reasons, but here are just a few:

"I was bored and gambling gave me something to do in an otherwise lonely existence."

"Gambling helped me forget the pain of my divorce."

"I told myself I was doing it for the money, but in reality it just helped me cope with stress.

"When I was younger I was highly successful. I had my first win and I was right back there."

"Gambling was a dreamworld where I was King. Everyone thought I was loaded. The only problem was that when I left, I was broke. "

"When I was gambling I felt like a winner, like I was successful as my brother."

"I lived on my own and had no-one or anything to do."

"It was some me-time after the kids had gone to bed. I used gambling to relax, although it ended up being highly stressful.

* * *

SUMMARY

We think we gamble to win, right? **Wrong.** It might have been like that once, but not anymore unfortunately.

These days, the only time you feel good, when your mind is working like it should, is when you're gambling. Gambling makes you feel whole again. Gambling is your norm. You need to feel like a Winner and On Top Of The World, to escape the feeling that some aspect of your life is out of control.

You use gambling to avoid and escape people, situations, problems, intimacy, and feelings.

Which is it for you?

QUIZ

How often do you walk away with money?
A: All the Time | Often | Not very Often | Hardly Ever

Chapter 4
How Did I Get Here?

When does a 'normal' Gambler cross the invisible line into becoming an 'abnormal' or 'problem' Gambler?

Firstly, let's define what actually IS 'normal' and what is not.

What is a Normal Gambler?

Anyone engaging in normal gambling can:

- Just have one or two bets, and not gamble until their last pound is gone
- Only stake money that was not intended for rent, food or bills
- Be honest about their whereabouts and what they were doing
- Generally be a truthful, reliable individual who shows consideration for others on a daily basis
- Have a reasonably multi-centred life with a mix of work, friends, relationship, family, sports and pastimes

A Problem Gambler – someone who gambles **abnormally** - is the complete *opposite* of this.

Remember those 20 Questions from earlier? A normal Gambler will put NO to most of them, if not all. Try it on your friends and family and see for yourself.

So where is this line? At what point do we cross over into irresponsible gambling, and start behaving like an Addict?

The Big Win

A common factor that most Gamblers report is that their gambling journey started with a win, usually a BIG win.

Amounts are irrelevant as they are proportional to earnings and lifestyle – a £100 win can be as significant to a Student as a £1000 win would be to a working person or as £10,000 to a business person or someone with money.

In that moment of the first Big Win, the Gambler's world lights up as they:

1. Have become the centre of attention
2. Realise they made the right choices
3. Feel the euphoria of their win
4. Might have made a profit

This last point is of course false, as they may have spent many hundreds or thousands in previous days or months. But they choose to ignore this in light of the Big Euphoric Win!

Even if they're playing online or at a machine, *they* know they've won. Everything lights up on screen in a mock celebration and confirms that they are successful. "YOU'VE WON!! YOU ARE A WINNER!" And in that perfect moment they can pay that bill, repay that debt, or have a chance of being normal. Their troubles are behind them. They are enough, even in their own eyes. They are a *winner*.

[They conveniently forget that they were actually normal before the gambling screwed them and their finances, but for now they are back on top for a change.]

However that feeling of being successful and worry free soon fades as the problem Gambler keeps going, rather than walking away.

Note that a 'Normal' Gambler CAN & often DOES cash out with their winnings, whereas an Abnormal Gambler just sees their winnings as a further stake (tokens, chips, credits, spins) for yet more gambling. They only feel at home in their own skin when they're in action.

They no longer see their winnings as money – their perception has been distorted by the addiction.

An Immature Mind

Gamblers seem to want all the good things in life without having to put the work in to get them. A common trait is that they are reluctant to grow up – often great fun to be around but completely unreliable.

They have little concept of the future, and what ideas they do have are massively over-optimistic. They keep telling themselves that they will succeed, or things will just work out, despite being aware of how their gambling behaviour is holding them back in many areas of their life.

- Subconsciously they want to avoid responsibility and struggle to take responsibility for their own acts

- They have an "all or nothing" attitude

- They expect special consideration and their feelings are easily hurt

- When criticised they get very defensive, sometimes aggressive

- Time has little relevance and they rely upon the inspiration of the moment

- They are the centre of the universe and everything revolves around them

AA, GA, NA and other anonymous groups include the "Definition of a Mature Person" in their literature (taken from a Los Angeles school programme) so clearly agree that immaturity is a major part of addiction. The idea is that if someone wants to recover from Gambling Addiction, then they must start behaving like a Mature Person (and over time become one).

So in our Daily Programmes section we have included a "Grown Up Checklist" for a list of less childish behaviours to strive for.

And later in the Science section we will find out WHY our brains haven't matured fully, and the underlying structural reason for it.

The Slippery Slope

The following pattern repeats itself more often than we care to admit, and despite our best efforts it always turns out the same:

- I **can't wait** to go back to see if I can win again

- I didn't win like the first time, but I probably will again – I won before so **I'm lucky**

- I'll try my luck again – I could use a bit of 'me' time

- I'm down a bit on last time so ideally **need to win it back**

- I've used up the last of my account so have borrowed from savings / partner / card / work

- I **need to go back** to see if I can win again

- I can't go back until payday, but can get a loan for food and rent (*let's hope I don't gamble it*)

- I can't tell my partner/family where I've been or what I've done, they'll kill me

- I can't pay for the mortgage / holiday / Birthday / Christmas - need to get money from somewhere

- I **need to go back** to see if I can **win big this time**

- Winning will pay my debts and solve all my problems

- Playing makes me *forget* about all my problems

In Their Own Words..

"The high came from just playing"

"I have been a problem gambler since my 18th Birthday, the first time I entered a casino. In that time, much like many others, I have lost thousands. Lost relationships, either directly or indirectly, almost been homeless, cried, lied, been so stressed and sad because of my utter inability to stop.

It started with Roulette, the quick fix, big win big loss game I'm sure we're all aware of. Spinning sometimes up to £1,000 in one spin. Once I confessed to my family about my problem after losing all my wages one month. I banned myself from local casinos, but then when the urge came back it just meant I had to drive a bit further.

Eventually for ease I would go to bookies. Losing thousands and winning thousands. Not being able to concentrate at work because all I wanted to do was spin that wheel, get money back that I'd lost, or increase amounts I had already won. To be honest, I don't ever think it really was about the winning or losing, the high came from just playing.

Fast forwarding a few years, the problem then became online slots, as well as scratchcards and football betting, and £1,000 bets on American sports, or horses, or dogs."

"Out of control"

"I'm out of control and push the boundaries beyond what is acceptable behaviour with my partner and unforgivable. Causes more problems as I have been using money that's not mine to gamble with. Yes it sounds down right blatant and doesn't give a toss behaviour! But I do!! I can't understand how I've allowed my morals to slip and cease to apply anymore. I have become totally numb mentally to the consequences of the need to gamble, when realistically I know the real situation and where I'm heading. And I'm scared and it really does feel hopeless."

"It's almost as if I lead a second life"

"I have been online gambling for 10 years now pretty much non-stop since my 18th birthday. It started off with online poker and then made its way into online sports betting. Over these 11 years I have lost countless amounts of money, put my parents through hell, lost friends, lost jobs and been generally lonely and on a slippery slope. Every month my wages would go in and within a day or two if I was lucky I would have lost all the wages and have to live the rest of the month without any money for food or to go out and do anything so I would be left sitting in my bedroom dying to get another bet on and then begging borrowing or stealing to get by. At 28 years old I basically have nothing to show for my life, a good education and 12 years of working and in debt, no real friends apart from my partner and can´t keep a roof over my head.

This month my wages went in as always on 31st July at midnight and by 8am they were gone. I now have no money for rent, or to pay back my mate who really needs back. I have decided enough is enough. I can´t live like this anymore. It's almost like I lead a second life. I have a great job, a loving family and a fantastic girlfriend. I am so close to losing all this if I cannot knock this evil demon on the head that I have let ruin my life for the last 11 years."

Lost it All

"I am 26 years old with a baby on the way. I have been gambling since was 17 and up until a couple of years it's always been relative amounts to what I can afford.

But a couple of years ago I started to gamble online and win big, between 2-4k and got the big buzz. Of course winning these amounts gets you into a mindset of 'I can win this all the time'.

Now I'm in a position where over the last 3 years I have probably lost 25k and I don't understand how it's just all happened so fast?

I know it's finally time to do something as last night I won 5k from £200 online within 4 hours and then went big and lost it all within an hour trying to go for the jackpot."

Affecting my Homelife

"I have been gambling for the last 6 years, but it has steadily got more and more of a problem and recently I am spending money I simply don't have. I have won/lost thousands over the years and I simply don't know what to do. I feel shaky and physically sick when I don't gamble and it's affecting my homelife."

Started in Pubs

"I started off on bandits in pubs, spending all my money for a night out on them, then I started playing the roulette games on the machines in the bookies and online. Recently roulette is where most of my money goes although I do have bets on the football and slots too. It has gotten to the stage where I think I'd bet on anything to get my fix. I just want to get better and be like I used to with confidence and always smiling and having a laugh."

Ran my Own Business

"I'm a web and graphic designer and I manage my own time. I can gamble whenever I want as I work alone. I wish I worked with others as it would save me from gambling. If I have just lost big, I get the next customer to pay – telling him the job was bigger than expected or invent some other problem."

"Yesterday while I was working I had £770 in my online betting account and lost all of it in basically 2 hours gambling on horses. Then I deposited another £765 from my bank and lost that in basically an hour trying to win back the £770 I originally had in my betting account. So basically in 3 hours I lost £1535. I really need to stop gambling as anything I ever win I just give it straight back to the bookmakers. There's days where I will gamble and just put a tenner on and be happy and enjoy a Saturday afternoon watching the racing. But when I have decent amounts of money available I just go and blow the lot and have like £300/£400 on one horse."

The Vicious Circle of Gambling

A teenager gambles online. He wins £50, and is rewarded with a HUGE surge of dopamine in his brain, a great reward feeling from gambling. He feels great.

The next time he feels bad, he wants to feel better and the idea of gambling pops into his head. But when he goes online and tries again, the great feeling doesn't happen. He keeps hoping and expecting it to happen though, and keeps gambling.

Soon he feels bad about the money he lost. The bad feeling drives him to look for a way to feel better, which activates the thought of more gambling. His subconscious mind is still referencing the high of the big win and how it made him feel, despite the interim losses.

Like this anyone can develop a gambling habit at any age, simply by using gambling to change the way they feel about themselves. But a *young brain* more easily builds neural highways big enough to outlast multiple disappointments.

Why? Neural pathways established within a developing teenage brain are more than just pathways – they are more like major *trunkroads or highways!* They are covered in insulating white brain matter (Myelin) which helps the neurons conducts electricity a lot faster than grey matter, just like RAM in your computer processes data way faster than a hard disk.

So Gambling Addiction developed in the teenage years is supported by well established, high speed circuitry that takes a little more effort to sort out than one developed later in life. But it can be done (I've done it).

Inevitable Outcomes

Listening to lived gambling experiences, you can quickly see the pattern of thought processes that go on inside a Gambler's mind throughout their addiction cycle. Gamblers always end up losing literally everything.

Sadly over the years I have known many Gamblers that have followed this exact path. As well as all their money, Gamblers lose their relationship, their home, and their job. They also lose other people's money, making it difficult for anyone to trust them again.

It's easy to see how gamblers lose their self-esteem and confidence, ending up an empty shell, sometimes homeless. They often become dual addicts self-medicating with drink and/or drugs to get them through the misery of losing everything. Others end up in prison where gambling is rife - not with money but with phone cards, tobacco and other supplies.

What started out as exciting entertainment and escape turned into an expensive nightmare that we can't afford. Meanwhile it hollows us out from the inside until we are numb and incapable of feeling proper emotions or maintaining loving relationships.

Perhaps you're at that point already, but too afraid to come clean and confront the consequences of your mess? Don't be - you can't manage the big secret forever. And the longer you keep a secret, the harder it is to talk about it. Secrets always come out eventually, and you'll get more sympathy if it comes out sooner as a voluntary confession rather than later as an unplanned discovery. *"I'll do it tomorrow"* isn't a practical strategy as you'll bottle out – talk to someone **today**, anyone. Once you start talking it gets easier.

And speaking as someone who has been where you are and has come through the other side, there IS hope. Yes it'll be messy in the short term - but not as messy as you think - and it *can* be sorted out. After they have got over their initial shock about being lied to or kept in the dark, people *will* help.

RockBottom

When talking about Addiction you always hear the phrase *"hitting rockbottom"* and the notion that someone cannot change until they've hit it. Only part of this is true, the part about finding a reason to change – that *"never again"* moment that will help motivate the person through the tough times.

But there is no actual 'rockbottom' as if you keep at it there is always somewhere lower you'll end up. Where are you on this ladder at the moment?

Lost my money
Lost my relationship
Lost my friends
Lost my job
Lost or left my home
Committed crime
Lost my freedom
Made bankrupt
Can no longer see my kids
Serious health problems
Living on the street, begging for food
Dead

Astonishingly the situation can & does get worse than that. Over the years I have known several people who have got through *multiple* relationships, *multiple* jobs and lost *multiple* homes – in other words, multiple rockbottoms.

So the painful experience of losing everything is not always a turning point. To a rational person maybe, but not to a compulsive Gambler who lives life in a distorted reality.

The trick is this. When you hit one of these levels, use that experience to get leverage on yourself - to say "NEVER AGAIN" - and then do <u>everything possible</u> to turn it around at that point.

Consider your current situation as a window of clear thinking - an opportunity to change, to say *never again*. Grab the opportunity, hold on with both hands, and don't let go. Do whatever it takes before it's too late.

Unhappy Endings

A Poorly Planned Robbery

I used to visit several Gamblers in prison. One particular guy (let's call him Mark) was inside for 18 months. After losing Mark had been desperate for money, but had never committed a crime. So he walked into a corner shop and when the lady opened the draw for change he waved a pocket penknife at her and tried to take the money from the till. She shut the cash register on Mark's fingers and he walked out. Or rather 'limped' out as he had a bad leg.

Mark had no car so literally limped a mile to his house with the £15 had got from the cash register. The shop owner followed him home on foot and called the police who came to arrest him. The judge gave Mark 3 years for robbery with aggravated assault. I visited him in prison every week for 18 months until he was released early.

Stress Relief

Steve used to gamble moderately but had a growing stress problem. Around 30 he got a job as a financial controller for a company in the Education sector. The business tripled in size from £1m to over £4m within just 3 years. But as the stress grew, so too did Steve's need for self-medication and escape. He used smaller amounts of company money to begin with, but he wasn't found out and these amounts got larger as his bets got larger – a lot bigger. He would "pay" himself into a dummy account £40,000 a time.

Several times he tried to quit, but the bookies sent him free all expenses trips to Dubai and other inducements in order to keep him as a VIP customer. The stress at work didn't let up so he would always revert back to gambling.

Several times he tried to talk to his employer about his stress, but never told them about the gambling for fear of the consequences. He eventually quit and the company called him a few months later to say that there was £250,000 missing from the accounts, and did he know anything about it. Steve told them it was a lot more than that – as much as £1million – and gave them bank statements. Steve was given a four year prison sentence and his wife and three young kids visit as often as they can. But Steve is remarkably positive about the experience and feels so much better now his secret is no longer a secret. He also intends to use his experiences to help others, and has already qualified as a Life Coach.

Couldn't Live with Himself

Another time I met a young mum. She said that her 30-year old husband and father of two young children had just killed himself. He was a school teacher and was collecting the kids Ski Trip money, but had a gambling problem which no-one knew about. You can guess the rest.

On the day he died, he kissed his wife goodbye as he was shaving in the bathroom. She said he seemed good within himself, better than normal in fact. Clearly he felt his options were narrowing and had decided that an early exit from this life was the only workable solution, which must have given him a sense of peace.

When she told me this, I assured her it was not her fault. But the doubt will always be there for her and their children who have to grow up without a father, always wondering if they were somehow to blame. How very sad and what a waste of life.

But it didn't need to be this way - he just couldn't see it at the time. The price of his life was probably in the region of £15,000 – around half his annual teaching salary - which could have easily been repaid over a few years.

Sadly, I have known a few parents of young adults that committed gambling-related suicide, which in the UK could be as many as 2 people A DAY. In almost every case the parent tells me they wish their child had met me and talked about their issue. Some of them owed as little as £2000 but to them it was a huge amount of money, and they felt hugely weighed down by the debt, lies, shame and seemingly inescapable cycle of despair. I usually reply it could have a been completely different story if they had just talked to someone – *anyone* – about their gambling problem. Without talking, things get completely out of proportion and perspective inside someone's head.

Even on the very day that I am sending this manuscript for publishing, a new message came in via my blog which reads:

> "I'm not a gambler .... but my son was. "Was" because he was killed in a car accident at the beginning of November and, in sorting out the aftermath of his death, I've discovered that he was gambling virtually everything he earned and everything he could borrow. I bailed him out of some debts 2 years ago and in the process discovered that he was gambling heavily. He gave me assurances that he would stop and I believed him. I didn't think that he was addicted as outwardly he led a normal life. I'm now tormented by so many "what if" questions and the most horrible thoughts of where his head was at the time of his accident. Keep up the good work so that you might help other parents avoid the kind of nightmare that I'm living."

* * *

Chapter 5
Why You Can NEVER Win

You're not going to like this, but there are five very good reasons why you can never, **ever** win at Gambling.

#1 – You Don't Gamble to Win

We already covered how you don't gamble to win. You're probably still arguing that fact, saying *"Don't be stupid, of COURSE I play to win - who doesn't?"*

Yes, you might *hope* you'll win. But the Problem Gambler - YOU - **gambles to gamble AGAIN**, to Stay in the Game. You plan and dream about it, look forward to the next session, and if truth be told, can't get enough of it. You get a buzz just *thinking* about it.

Winning prolongs your play time, which is why you frequently gamble longer than you planned. And you lose all track of time too.

#2 – You Ignore the <u>Real</u> Odds of winning

Take the simple example of a coin toss. We toss the coin 7 times and it lands *Heads* each time. We might think that it MUST be a Tails soon based on previous history of it being Heads. But in reality the odds are still 50%, ie. 1/2 as they have always been on each coin toss.

This is known as *The Gamblers Fallacy* or the Monte Carlo Fallacy where in a casino in 1913 it was first noted that a roulette ball fell in black 26 times in a row. On that occasion Gamblers lost millions of francs betting against black, reasoning incorrectly that the streak was causing an imbalance in the randomness of the wheel, and that it had to be followed by a long streak of red.

#3 – It's A Rigged Game.

Most gamblers believe that the longer you play and haven't won, the closer you are to winning. This logic is completely **wrong**. Each type of gambling is subtly different, but they are all rigged in some respect so that the House <u>always</u> wins. Ask yourself:

> *"How much have I WON*
> *in the last 3 months, approximately? [Be honest]*
> *And how much of those winnings do I have now?"*
>
> Did you just say: "I won, but put in all back in again?

This is why the UK Gambling Industry has grown to a massive £14Billion pounds within just a few years. That's **Fourteen-THOUSAND-Million-Pounds...** £38million a day... **£1.6m a minute.**

On each Electronic Gambling Machine or online simulation you will usually see the letters 'RTP' and a percentage. This stands for "Return to Player" and is known amongst players as the average payout.

Most players believe that if the RTP is say 70%, then for every £1 staked they should get around 70p back? False.

The RTP figure is in fact calculated and averaged out over hundreds, thousands or even *tens of thousands* of spins. So if a Gambler has played on a machine for say 3 hours and it has not paid out, then staying on the machine for a further 3 hours or even 3 days will do very little to improve their chances of winning!

But for you, the Problem Gambler, the general takeaway is this:

(1) Both Electronic Gambling Machines and online simulated machines are simply running programs, and the Operator always wins (by design). The game is programmed so that THEY WIN, YOU LOSE. This is why they make so much money – a staggering £1.6million a minute for every minute of every day, 24/7, all year round. No wonder the CEO of Bet365 pays herself an average bonus of £250 million a year, on top of her salary! The house is only winner, and

you have personally paid towards the CEO's bonus or her shiny new luxury car.

(2) Each time you play you might *think* you have a good chance of winning, but in reality you don't - unless you gambled for a year, 365 days straight without a break. And even then you'd be lucky to see 70% back of what you paid out.

[see Appendix V for more detail on RTP]

#4 - You Chase Your Losses

A hallmark of a Problem Gambler is that they chase their losses with yet more money, and when they win can't walk away.

Gamblers always justify their actions to themselves as the correct course of action:

"I'm already [X] down and I've got to win it back"

"That money was for rent, I've got to win it back"

"My luck's got to change soon, I'll ride it out"

"I always get there eventually"

"I've been tracking the patterns and know it's going to pay out soon"

"I know the system, I'll win soon"

"I'm on a roll!"

"I've got half my salary back, I need to keep going and get the other half"

"My luck's changing, I can win more"

"I've cracked the system – I can clean up now"

"I've spotted the sequence – it's definitely going to payout now, I'm certain"

"If I keep winning, I'll be able to pay ALL my debts and be free at last!"

"If I win big this time, I can look after everybody"

If you chase your losses, and can't walk away with your winnings, face facts: it's a NO-WIN Situation – every single time.

But even now you're thinking *"If only I could find a way ..."* But you can't or you would have done it by now, right? And you'd be reading this in your mansion sipping cocktails by your pool, correct?

#5 – You are Psychologically *Unable* to Stop

We're going to cover this in detail in the next chapter, but essentially an important part of your brain that makes all your key decisions - the **Prefrontal Cortex** - actually SHUTS DOWN during your gambling sessions.

This means you are unable to process normal questions in your head, like:

Should I continue?"

I'm already at my limit, should I call it a day?

This is the food money - if I lose what are we going to eat?

How am I going to get home?

Once you start gambling, you quite literally *CANNOT STOP* until you run out of credit or they kick you out. You are hurtling along, a passenger in your own car, and no-one is at the wheel.

* * *

SUMMARY

The odds of winning are stacked vastly in favour of the Gambling Operator and against the Gambler. Addicts choose to ignore logic in order to get their buzz and stay in the game.

If we LOSE we chase our losses and dig a bigger hole. And if we WIN we want to win more and can't bring ourselves to quit while we're ahead. It literally is a NO-WIN situation.

The punchline is that when we get going, part of our brain actually shuts down, making it *impossible* for us to make the decision to stop!

We may as well just empty our pockets and flush the money down the toilet.

What We've Learned So Far...

Here's a quick recap.

1. We recognise that we always spend more *Money* that we planned, and spend more *Time* that we planned, and that gambling is causing growing problems in our life.

2. We considered a definition of problem gambling as *"something that a person enjoys, finds relief in, and craves in the short term but suffers negative consequences in the long term, and doesn't give up despite the negative consequences."*

3. In the 20 questions you worked out if you either *ARE* or *ARE NOT* a Compulsive Gambler. If you've any doubt then go back over the 20 questions and answer them honestly this time. Accepting that you have a problem is our starting point.

4. We learned that we use Gambling to escape into our Dreamworld or Bubble, promising ourselves that this time it's going to be different (but it never is).

5. Gambling Addiction isn't the primary problem, it's an *attempt to solve* a problem.

6. Gamblers don't gamble to win, we gamble to stay in the game, to keep playing. This was a tough one but deep

down we know it to be true. We looked at examples of how others use gambling.

7. We looked at the Big Win (whether at the start or elsewhere on our gambling journey) and saw what it did for us, and how our brain is always trying to get us back there.

8. We looked at the various stages on the Slippery Slope that we've all been down, and identified with some personal gambling stories.

9. We looked at the vicious circle of gambling, and how it inevitably ends up the same way despite our best efforts. We also looked at rockbottom and saw how there is always somewhere *lower* we can go, until we finally decide to enough is enough and take proper decisive action.

10. To cap it off, we thought about why problem gamblers can never win as:

We don't gamble to win & walk away, we gamble to keep playing
We ignore the real odds in order to keep playing and to stay in our bubble
It's a rigged game where the house always wins - we may as well just empty our pockets or flush our money down the toilet
A key part of our brain actually *shuts down* and we are *unable* to decide to stop or walk away
(more on that in the next chapter)

THE SCIENCE

BEHIND

WHY

YOU GAMBLE
ABNORMALLY

Chapter 6
A Misfiring Brain

The first fact that we must get our heads around is that Addiction (whether to a substance or a behaviour) is a *Biological* Process. Every behaviour we have is a result of the way in which our brain functions.

With the help of modern MRI and EEG scanners, we can now actually *see* different areas of the brain attempting to process addictive thoughts and act out on them, while other parts of the brain are not as active as they would normally be.

Your Amazing Brain

Our brains are capable of processing **30 Billion bits** of information **a second** and consist of around **6,000 miles** of wiring. Typically the human nervous system contains around **28 Billion** *neurons* (nerve cells designed to conduct impulses). Each one of these neurons can handle around **1 Million bits of information,** and each neuron connects to others to make up small neural networks (which in turn combine together to carry out larger operations).

It's a modular, highly efficient design - a result of millions of generations (cycles of evolution) where only things that work make it into the next version.

Addiction Changes the Natural Balance

All biological systems attempt to maintain a normal balance, known as *homeostasis*. The brain functions as the overseer of this balance. It makes various adjustments to maintain a balanced, well-functioning, biological system – body temperature, body fluid composition, blood sugar, gas concentrations, and blood pressure.

Each person's normal balance is individually determined, but behavioural addictions like gambling and substance abuse lead to changes in this normal balance. The part of the brain that handles this balance is the *Hypothalamus*, our Maintenance Man (or "Janitor" as I refer to him in the book).

Chronic over-stimulation of the brain (which occurs with gambling addiction) interferes with the maintenance of this balance. When the brain has difficulty maintaining homeostatic balance, our wonderfully adaptive brain makes adjustments. It does this by creating a new balanced set-point, via a process called *allostasis*.

It's a bit like losing your hearing. This would create an immediate disorientation as you rely on your hearing to give you information about the world and what's going on around you. But because the brain adapts, it instructs your other senses to step up and compensate. Your sight becomes keener, as does your sense of smell. You sense vibration more in your body. You learn to read lips in order to receive verbal communication.

And behind the scenes in your brain, the neural pathways that govern those other senses are all automatically recalibrating themselves to meet the new demands placed upon them. And soon you have a new personal normal - normal for *you*.

The body works in a similar way. You lift weights which creates a response in your body to build muscle, so it can adapt and lift the load more easily in future. Carrying more muscle and having more power is the new normal. Both your body and your brain constantly recalibrate what is normal (for you).

Maintaining the New Balance at All Costs

Our brain's primary survival need to maintain *homeostasis* - balance - can result in unwanted side effects:

1) The powerful need to obtain drugs or continue harmful activities, despite the harm to self or loved ones

2) The withdrawal symptoms and difficulty in quitting an addictive activity or drug

3) The obsessive, all-consuming nature of addictions - little else in life matters.

This is because addiction caused the brain's balance to change, in order to accommodate the addiction. Just like an alcoholic might need half a bottle of whiskey before he feels himself and can function, it's the same with you and the gambling.

Once changed, the brain _requires_ the addictive activity or substance in order to maintain this new homeostatic balance. I might THINK that my brain is telling me that I need gambling / cocaine / alcohol / whatever just to get me through the day, but actually it is telling me that it needs [*my drug of choice*] so that my brain can be in *balance* and therefore has a *chance of coping* with the demands of the day. It is my crutch which my brain tells me I need in order to walk.

Neurotransmitters - The Brain's Own Drug Supply

A drug addict will inject/ingest foreign substances directly into their system in order to feel a change of state, to escape from themselves.

But anyone with a *behavioural* addiction - Gambling, Porn, Food, Gaming, Shopping, etc - can trick their brain into producing its OWN drugs which change the owner's state, allowing them to escape from themselves.

These "drugs" are the neurotransmitters Dopamine, Noradrenaline, Serotonin and Endorphins – the behavioural addict's cocktail of choice.

Serotonin - reduces anxiety, increases sense of well-being
Dopamine - increases confidence, focus and energy
Noradrenaline - increases focus, energy and strength
Endorphins - reduces stress, soothes pain for injury or fatigue

Here is a visual representation of the different chemical interactions and the jobs they perform.

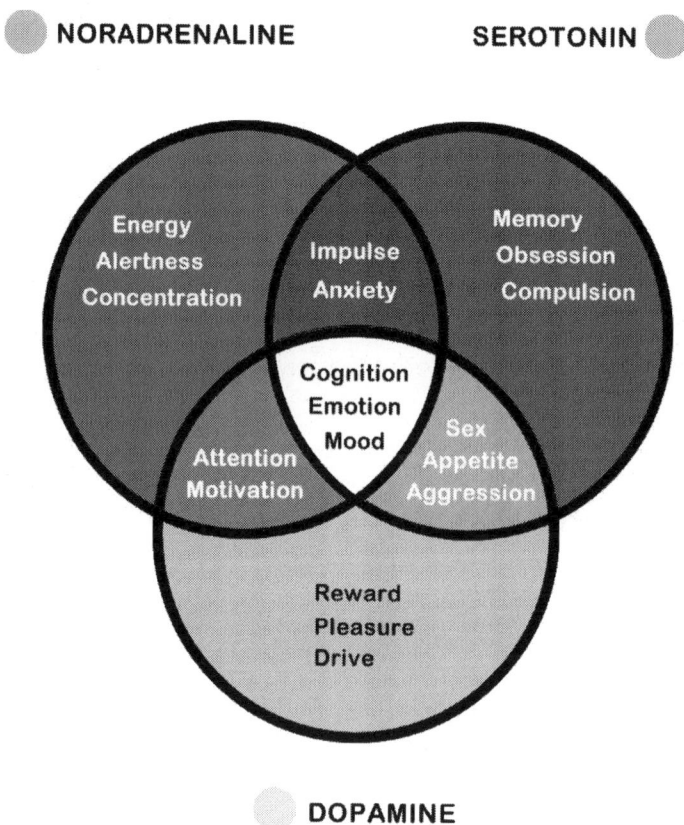

NORADRENALINE   SEROTONIN

Energy
Alertness
Concentration

Impulse
Anxiety

Memory
Obsession
Compulsion

Cognition
Emotion
Mood

Attention
Motivation

Sex
Appetite
Aggression

Reward
Pleasure
Drive

DOPAMINE

A Quick Chemistry Lesson

The human brain is a chemical supercomputer that learns and rewires itself based on its rewards (and perceived rewards). It has a number of unique characteristics that have ensured our evolution and survival over millions of years.

As a Gambler you feel *up* and *down*, *depressed* and *on top of the world*. These chemicals in your brain explain why.

Brain Chemicals => **Emotions, Thoughts & Feelings**

NORADRENALINE

Noradrenaline (also known as Norepinephrine) mobilises the brain & body for action. It reaches high levels during situations of stress or danger, in the *fight-or-flight* response. Noradrenaline increases arousal & alertness in the brain, promotes vigilance, enhances formation & retrieval of memory, and focuses attention. It also increases restlessness, anxiety, and increases heart rate & blood pressure.

Low Noradrenaline results in:

- Lack of energy
- Lack of motivation
- Lack of focus and attention
- Sleeping too much
- Depressed mood

DOPAMINE

A neurotransmitter that helps control the brain's reward & pleasure centres. Helps regulate movement and emotional responses.

Abnormally high levels of dopamine are linked to loss of contact with reality, delusions and lack of emotion, while low levels have been associated with addictive behaviour and risk taking.

Dopamine enables us not only to see and get excited about rewards, but to take action to move toward them.

Normal people get *rewarded* with Dopamine when they get Creative or Productive:

1. Discovering new things
2. Listing down small tasks & ticking them off a daily ToDo list
3. Listening to music
4. Exercising often
5. Establishing a streak (maintaining a productive task on an ongoing basis)

Note that the brain releases Dopamine when the reward is simply **anticipated**. This is massively important, as the gambling brain rewires itself based on what it thinks it *will* win, rather than historically what it has lost. A gambler starts to get a buzz just *thinking* about gambling later in the day.

See this in realtime in the astonishing BBC documentary where Professor David Nutt puts a Problem Gambler in a MRI Scanner and asks him to gamble (see blog for details).

This is like Pavlov's dog who was trained to salivate when it simply *heard* the bell for food, even though the food had not appeared yet. Clinical tests on pathological Gamblers have shown they also literally start to salivate in their mouths at simply *watching* a video of gambling.

Low Dopamine symptoms are:

- Lack of pleasure
- Lack of optimism about future events
- Inability to feel excited
- Feeling more irritable than low serotonin does
- Waking up in the middle of the night

The main difference between lack of Dopamine and lack of Serotonin (next) is that with lack of just Dopamine there is often a complete absence of anxiety.

SEROTONIN

A chemical nerve that cells produce and sends signals between your nerve cells.

90% of your body's Serotonin can be found in your digestive system, but also in blood platelets & throughout the entire central nervous system. It helps regulate your mood naturally.

Gambling causes *Stress* which in turn depletes Serotonin.

Low levels of Serotonin cause:

- Anxiety – feeling of unease in oneself, on edge
- Low self-confidence - most noticeable in situations requiring larger groups of people
- Digestive problems - stomach cramps, sensitivity
- Poor sleep quality - waking up feeling tired and cranky
- Increased irritability - verges on aggression at times, snapping at people

But when your Serotonin levels are normal, you feel:

- Happier
- Calmer
- More focused
- Less anxious
- More emotionally stable

ENDORPHINS

Endorphins are natural opioids, produced by the body in response to pain, excitement and even exercise.

Endorphins is actually short for "Endogenous Morphine" meaning *"morphine produced naturally in the body"*. Yes, our clever brain creates its own morphine.

Endorphin binds to the same receptors as the pain-relieving drug morphine. These receptors, present on nerves in the brain and spinal cord, modulate the activity of nerves, causing mild sedation, relieving pain and giving a sense of wellbeing and euphoria. Exercise and Yoga will trigger endorphins.

Note to Self:

The best ARTIFICIAL way to boost Serotonin, Noradrenaline, Dopamine and Endorphins together is **Gambling**. But it is a massively expensive way, and also generates Cortisol (stress) which causes problems for the heart and nervous system. Takes years off your life.

The best NATURAL way to boost Serotonin, Noradrenaline, Dopamine and Endorphins together is by doing **Cardiovascular Exercise** – all of the benefits with none of the cost! No stress, heart healthy, and adds years onto your life.

Two other backstage characters worth an honourable mention are:

OXYTOCIN

Often described as the *"bonding"* hormone, the *"trust"* hormone, or sometimes even the *"love"* hormone, oxytocin is unique to mammals. Although research is still in its infancy, Oxytocin is thought to play an important role in human intimacy, childbirth, sexual arousal, trust and pair bonding. But Gamblers literally *bond* with machines and screens. We are literally *in love* with gambling, a mistress we spend a great deal of time and money on.

GABA

Gamma Amino Butyric Acid (GABA) is the main inhibitory Neurotransmitter in the brain. It decreases nerve transmission, allowing neurons time to recover. Increased GABA activity in the brain relieves anxiety and reduces stress. GABA helps keep Dopamine levels in check.

Behavioural Addicts Make their Own Drugs

Anyone addicted to substances obviously injects or ingests foreign substances directly into their system, in order to feel a change of state or escape.

But a behavioural addict like a Gambler can trick or deliberately stimulate the body into producing its OWN drugs – chemicals - which then change the person's state:

- Gambling, Porn, Cocaine, and Food all stimulate the release of Dopamine & Serotonin.

- Even the ANTICIPATION of any of the above is enough to start the production of these chemicals.

The Addict eventually gets sick of the substance (while requiring more & more of it to create the same high) as the brain adapts and becomes harder to trick as plasticity increases.

But being sick is not enough to change the underlying destructive behaviour patterns, and the gambler must find new ways to get the same high. After upping their bets to very large amounts to achieve this, they might also try new games or apps, or might even switch stimulants altogether to Cocaine, Porn or Alcohol to fool their savvy brain.

Over the years I have known many gamblers that have had multiple addictions. But in reality, they only have ONE addiction with multiple manifestations.

Remember:

ADDICTION ISN'T THE PRIMARY PROBLEM
*IT'S **AN ATTEMPT TO SOLVE** A PROBLEM*

You may be in recovery for one addiction, but if the underlying problem is still there then more addictions will most likely follow. Avoid and escape are the hallmarks of addiction.

The Gambler's High

Inside a Gambler's brain there is no longer anything remotely normal about the production & regulation of Noradrenaline, Dopamine & Serotonin.

From an evolutionary point of view, the brain's reward system ensured our survival. We are more likely to repeat behaviours that are pleasurable.

To recap, the chemical manipulation starts way before the first bet. Just *thinking* about going gambling will start the release of the various chemicals in the brain. Even *watching* someone gambling stimulates an effect I have heard referred to as "secondary gambling" where your brain lights up as if it was actually gambling! This follows the old patterns (*neural pathways*) and re-enforces them, like a well-worn path through a forest. Just like one of Pavlov's dogs, we mentally start to salivate just at the *thought* of gambling. Hopefully you have watched the gambler going into an MRI scanner and thinking about gambling (see blog for details).

And once the first bet is placed, those original feelings surge like a tsunami as *memories of wins* and associated *patterns of significance* are recalled into the mind & body.

- **Adrenaline** is released and their heart starts to pound with the ancient *'Fight or Flight'* response. But the Gambler finds this danger challenging, exciting & exhilarating and never runs the other way. As an adrenaline junkie, it's all part of the game.

- MASSIVE amounts of **Dopamine** and **Serotonin** are released, washing over the brain over the course of the gambling session. This session might last anything from a *few minutes* to a *few hours* to even *several days*.

- **Cortisol** stress hormone is also released as the Gambler loses, and they attempt to get more wins (Dopamine) to make the feeling go away. Deep in the centre of the brain, the *Amygdala* - an almond-shaped set of neurons responsible for managing Emotions & Memory - becomes overloaded with Stress.

In animal studies excess Cortisol has been shown to cause important brain centres (*like the Prefrontal Cortex*) to shrink and not function as well, sometimes to shut down completely.

Cortisol is also responsible for stopping the production of new neurons in the *Hippocampus*, the part of the brain that stores memories. This can affect decision making, working memory and control of impulsive behaviour. Cortisol also stops the production of brain-derived neurotrophic factor (BDNF). This is a protein that keeps brain cells healthy and forms new ones. The gambler is chock solid with Cortisol, giving them stress and brain freeze.

> *We become addicted to the **chemicals***
> *that our brain releases*
> *and the way in which they make us feel.*
>
> *NOT the substance or activity*
> *that causes this release.*

The Gambling Hangover

Once the gambling has stopped, the Adrenaline & Dopamine rollercoaster is replaced with heavy feelings of Guilt & Fear. Reality bites.

The Gambler emerges into the cold light of day or turns off their device. As the numbness wears off, reality hits them hard, and so too the awful realisation that they have made the problem *worse* not better. They feel the fear of being found out and experience the massive stress of not being to pay bills or debts, or even eat. They are in a bigger mess than before, and more desperate too.

After a long gambling session, the Gambler may not have eaten for a long time. The adrenaline has left their system and blood sugar will be low. So they need another hit to bring them back up, like sugar or alcohol. They will certainly avoid other people and turn off their phone to avoid questions they can't answer.

At this point they promise themselves
that was the VERY last time,
and never to gamble again.

But their Gambler brain is hard wired to follow the same established pathways. Consequentially the person is unable to see their promise through, even with the best of intentions. *Willpower* is Not Enough. Their behaviour is dictated by their brain's programming that compels them to act this way, time after time. And with each repetition of gambling that wiring becomes stronger too, making it stronger and more robust.

But there is SO much more to the story than just Dopamine and other brain chemicals. Most people have missed what's really going on inside a Gambler's brain, and believe me it's quite astonishing.

Gambling like a Zombie

When in action the Gambler is literally **brain-washed** with these Noradrenaline, Dopamine, Serotonin and Endorphin hormones and all reason goes out of the window. They will gamble their entire months' wages, without even the money to get home and nothing to pay rent or buy food until next payday. Why?

Well it's more than just an overload of neurotransmitters. In fact, it's probably the most significant fact that has ever been discovered about why Problem Gamblers can't seem to stop themselves, when others can.

It's a little-known fact, but Problem Gamblers are physiologically UNABLE to_stop, as the part of the brain that would allow them to make the decision to stop has been temporarily hindered and often DISABLED altogether.

"The frontal lobe literally shuts down," said psychologist Heather Chapman, who directs the Brecksville VA Medical Centre's gambling treatment programme.

*"The prefrontal cortex is like the 'Mom or Dad' of the brain. It helps us make good decisions -- you've had enough, it's time to go home. That literally has been shown to **shut down** in the pathological gambler, as it is in Cocaine users."*

During the Problem Gambler's session, the **Prefrontal Cortex** - the brain's decision making centre - SHUTS DOWN impairing the brain's ability to decide that enough is enough. *So once a Problem Gambler is in action, they are unable to call it a day.*

Read that again and see if you can take it in - I had trouble the first time I read it. We are physiologically incapable of deciding to stop. Maybe normal people that have moderate gambling habits can stop, yes - but not us. The part of our brain that is able to call time and say "*enough is enough*" has gone offline.

The gambling session therefore only stops when the money runs out, or when the Gambler is unable to obtain money by some other means (ie. raid other accounts or borrow etc) or when they are physically dragged away or summoned... or when the betting shop closes and kicks them out.

Incidentally these symptoms are *identical* to Crack Cocaine and Crystal Meth addicts. The brain scans of Cocaine and Gambling Addicts are usually identical in this regard. So if you think that being a Gambling Addict is somehow better than being hooked on Crack, you'd be wrong.

That kind of unregulated, unstoppable behaviour seems *insane* to a normal person. "*Why don't they just stop?*" they say. But to the Gambler's mind this is normal, as their circuits are wired that way and reinforced with every all-or-nothing gambling session. They are used to their brain going numb in a drugged trance-like state, and actually *like* it as it gives them escape from their problems. They are in their Dreamworld, their Bubble.

With the Prefrontal Cortex shut down, no one is in control. You're on autopilot, shovelling money into a machine or screen, or placing bets behind a counter, or sitting in a casino in a trance betting on anything. This is why gamblers often admit they were no longer in control... well, they actually weren't. They went through several red lights with nobody at the wheel.

The insurance report might read something like this:

> **"Simply driving the car caused Failure of the Engine Management System - resulting in sudden and complete brake failure** (and subsequent harm to the driver, who was unaware of the risks)."

And we can now see why 'normal' thoughts and values go out of the window. If the decision-making part of the brain is offline, normal sensible thoughts CANNOT occur, thoughts like:

"Should I continue?"

"I'm already at my limit, should I call it a day?"

"This is my food money, should I continue?"

"I've just gambled the mortgage money and might lose my house, should I stop?"

"If I spend this, how am I going to get home?"

As you have probably realised by now, willpower and reason have nothing to do with it, whatsoever.

I remember one gambler - let's call him Paul - a nicer guy you couldn't hope to meet. Bright too, having a top job as a public servant. But Paul used to have a gambling problem, betting shops mainly. He used to 'pop out to get the milk' etc and go to the betting shop on a Saturday afternoon. Being on 'Dad' duty and not wishing to arouse suspicion he used to take the kids with him in the car, 3 and 5yr old, and would park right outside the bookies.

But one bet led to another, 10 minutes turned into half an hour, and he would return to the car after an hour or two (3 hours on one occasion) after he had run out of money. The kids would be in a right state – hungry, fighting, wet themselves, in general chaos. I remember the look of shame on Paul's face as he spoke of these things. He said that his youngest had now developed a facial twitch and had anger / abandonment issues. He could even develop ADD and go on to become an Addict himself (see later).

Gambling is a mental health issue. Paul's story was 22 years ago but is still an everyday occurrence. Why? Because Industry, Government and law makers have not yet fully grasped WHAT Gambling Addiction is, and HOW it affects us.

Other Interesting Facts about the PFC

I appreciate that that finding out that a key part of our brain has been failing repeatedly is a lot to get our heads around – it was for me. When I realised this, it all started to made sense. I wasn't insane after all.

But to get a handle on the full gravity of the situation, just have a look at ALL the jobs the PFC does and what decisions it is responsible for. Then think about what would happen to *your* life if your prefrontal cortex was inhibited or completely offline for any period of time.

Executive Human Brain Functions

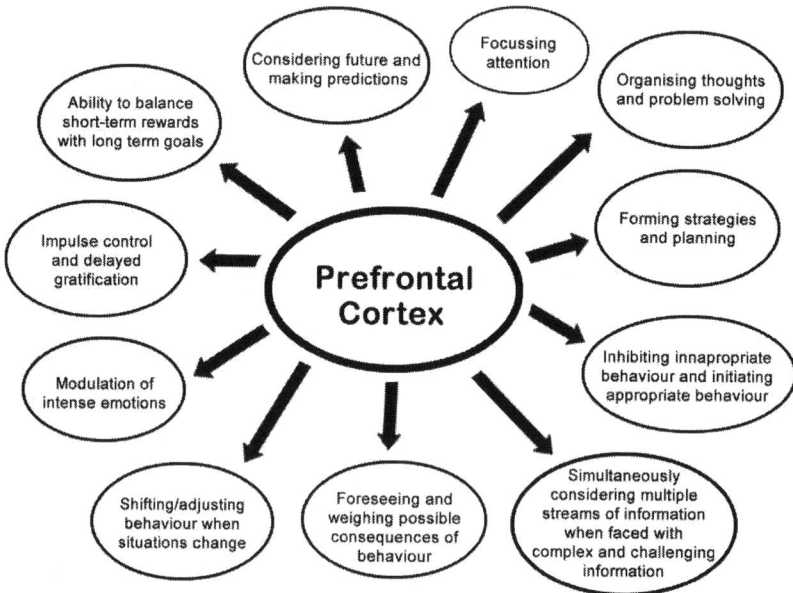

Diagram showing the Prefrontal Cortex at the centre with arrows pointing to the following functions: Considering future and making predictions; Focussing attention; Organising thoughts and problem solving; Ability to balance short-term rewards with long term goals; Forming strategies and planning; Impulse control and delayed gratification; Inhibiting innapropriate behaviour and initiating appropriate behaviour; Modulation of intense emotions; Shifting/adjusting behaviour when situations change; Foreseeing and weighing possible consequences of behaviour; Simultaneously considering multiple streams of information when faced with complex and challenging information.

Did you specifically notice these functions?

- *Forming strategies and planning*
- *Impulse control and delaying gratification*
- *Considering the future and making predictions*

76

- *Foreseeing and weighing possible consequences of behaviour*

It's no wonder that gamblers destroy themselves when they are gambling. All their good intentions didn't go out of the window - they simply went to sleep while the damage was occurring. Just like if your body suffers massive sudden impact, you don't feel the pain as your brain uses *shock* – an ancient survival mechanism - to anesthetise you.

And ironically, when later questioned by the partner why they gambled everything away, the Gambler's answer "*I don't know*" was actually true.

Also consider the following facts about the Prefrontal Cortex:

1. Our PFC doesn't mature until the age of **25**. This explains why teenagers try things with little regard for safety, common sense, etc and make some very impulsive and questionable decisions. In many ways Problem Gamblers are *immature teenagers* that never grew up – I certainly was. Do you remember the mention of Immaturity earlier? We'll come back to this later on.

2. Repeated behaviours in teenage years don't just form ordinary neural networks in their brains – they are more like *super-circuits*, insulated with white brain

matter (Myelin) to make them super-conductive and super-efficient. Addiction developed before the age of 25 therefore has more neural infrastructure behind it than addiction developed later in life.

3. The PFC in people diagnosed with ADD (Attention Deficit Disorder) is *smaller* and *less developed* than in people without ADD. So even before the shutdown that we experience when we are gambling, people with ADD are already have a smaller amount of neurons doing the job (like a smaller CPU in a computer) and therefore more prone to making bad decisions. You'll learn more about ADD later, and maybe find out that you have undiagnosed ADD (like me).

4. THE PFC *shuts down* during gambling. I remember vividly how *numb* my mind always felt, sitting in front of screen in a hypnotised trance, like it wasn't me. Time had no meaning and I would gamble for hours and hours, sometimes all day and all night. Money had no meaning and I would put more in and go again. Repeat 500 times. Looking back, I knew I wasn't all there. But now through my research I now <u>SCIENTIFICALLY KNOW WHY</u> I wasn't all there! I've included links to further research in the Appendix VI in case anyone wants to know more.

If the PFC's Offline, Who's in Charge?

It's not strictly true so say *"no-one's at the wheel"* – it's way worse than that. When our Executive Decision centre shuts down, control is passed to the *Amygdala* and *Hypothalamus*, both centres in the older part of our brain that work very differently and that govern entirely separate functions.

The brain has been evolving for millions of years. As Apes we developed the **Limbic System** which reacts only to drives and instincts that we experience as *feelings and impressions*. Then as we evolved into walking, talking, thinking Humans we developed the **Frontal Cortex**, which deals with *facts, logic and reason.*

Both brains exist, one inside the other, and are essential to everyday function and survival. While the more recent *"human"* brain is capable of logically evaluating information and making calm, rational decisions, the older *"chimp"* brain makes blazing fast emotional and instinctive responses, and can throw the occasional tantrum and be pretty disruptive (especially when under stress and overloaded).

If the Prefrontal Cortex is the thinking, rational *CEO* of our Company brain, then the Hypothalamus is the *Maintenance Man* whose job it is to maintain the brain's **balance** (*homeostasis*) no matter what. He normally makes sure all the utilities like body temperature, hunger, thirst, and sleep are running correctly... and produces Dopamine.

Meanwhile the Amygdala is a Chimp that runs our **Emotion** centre where she instinctively manages Fear, Pleasure, Anxiety and Anger. She doesn't think, she feels and reacts. And when she's overloaded she's not exactly stable. Ever seen a stressed-out chimp?

So while your CEO is offline and unavailable, these guys are running the company. The lunatics have just taken over the asylum – the Janitor and a stressed-out chimp who is overloaded and emotionally unstable due to what we are doing to her.

"When things are going well, the prefrontal cortex acts as a control centre that keeps our baser emotions and impulses in check. The new research demonstrates that acute, uncontrollable stress sets off a series of chemical events that weaken the influence of the prefrontal cortex while strengthening the dominance of older parts of the brain. In essence, it transfers high-level control over thought and emotion from the prefrontal cortex to the *hypothalamus* and *other earlier evolved structures*. As the older parts take over, we may find ourselves either consumed by paralyzing anxiety or else subject to impulses that we usually manage to keep in check: indulgence in excesses of food, drink, drugs or a spending spree at a local specialty store.

Quite simply, we lose it."

[Amy Arnsten, Carolyn M. Mazure, and Rajita Sinha, see Appendix on PFC for full article]

"Conditions such as anxiety, autism, depression, post-traumatic stress disorder, and phobias are suspected of being linked to abnormal functioning of the Amygdala owing to *damage, developmental problems,* or *neurotransmitter imbalance.*"

[Science Daily]

It's also worth noting that in other studies, activating the Amygdala in rats **intensifies motivation** to consume cocaine far beyond ordinary drug levels. This is similar to its ability to intensify motivation for sweet foods such as sugar. *"Rats were also willing to work almost three times harder for the cocaine when paired with Amygdala activation"* the study indicates.

Without our rational human CEO telling us to call it a day and an aggressive anxious Chimp running the show, we increase our bets and take more risk without thinking. All preset limits are meaningless. We empty wallets, cards, bank accounts, get payday loans, and do all that as well until we are completely dry.

We literally bet everything for a banana.

Storing Triggers on Speed Dial

As well as Emotion, the Amygdala is associated with memory and stores certain "*cues*" as positive or negative memories. For a simple example, let's suppose a man stops at an ATM every day after a work. He withdraws £20, which the machine delivers as a single £20 note. He takes this note to the local shop to buy scratchcards. The ATM, £20 notes, the shop, and the time after work now serve as cues or *"triggers"* to gamble. This is because these cues are stored as a positive memory associated with gambling, more so if he wins.

So while the PFC is shut down and our CEO decision-maker is offline, our inner chimp is recording and referencing all the emotion connected with the gambling, still trying to get her *"banana"* with a win. She feels the Fear and Anxiety and intuitively sees this as her solution.

Meanwhile the Hypothalamus (our Janitor) is pumping out Dopamine to make everything happy which in turn creates problems with stress regulation.

A Massively Misunderstood Condition

Even as I write these facts, I am stunned by them. For years people have not wanted to talk about Gambling Addiction due to the stigma. It's described as an *illness*, a *disease* and there is so much *shame*. Of course nobody wants to put their hand up and admit it. People walk into recovery groups and therapy centres hanging their heads, apologising for their very existence.

And yet when we look at Gambling Addiction from a purely scientific perspective, it is simply a symptom of an underdeveloped Prefrontal Cortex, or one that has been washed with so much Adrenaline and Cortisol (stress) that it has gone into shutdown and responsibility has transferred to other parts of the brain, less skilled for the job and with more basic priorities.

No wonder gamblers "wake up" full of despair after a session and can't believe the damage they've done while they were "asleep"! So much guilt and remorse. It's no wonder that we are seeing more and more gambling-related suicide.

> **It's like having a nightmare, then waking in the morning to find you actually committed the crime - questioning who the hell you are and what you must be capable of doing**

Society certainly has little current understanding of this. I doubt a judge has ever heard of an underdeveloped

'Prefrontal Cortex' or 'ADD' in relation to a gambling crime. Too often the focus on is the crime and the actions of the addict to fuel their addiction, rather than identifying WHY they were addicted – due to an underdeveloped brain, or a temporary brain condition caused by prolonged massive neurotransmitter stimulation. Rather than sending such people to prison, we should be treating this as a **Mental Health issue** and recommending an appropriate course of treatment. (see Appendix VII for further information)

And what of the Gambling Operators, who make a vast proportion of their profits from a small amount of people who are literally unable to stop, not even if they wanted to? These people open their wallets every payday and the Operators take their money willingly, often seeing huge amounts being gambled in relation to that customer's previous betting amounts and frequency. *Could the PFC be the next PPI?*

And certainly most Gambling Addiction therapies don't address it from this angle. If you had an underdeveloped leg which was weak and causing you to limp, you might be prescribed some physio and leg strengthening exercises to make it stronger. And after 8 weeks, no more limp – maybe even stronger than before. Problem, Solution.

So why not take the same approach with mental exercises to strengthen the weak or underdeveloped areas of the brain? Seems obvious to me.

Neuroplasticity – A Self Wiring Brain

Just like the muscle, the human brain has the amazing capability to adapt itself to the demands that are being place upon it. When we undertake a new task, new connections are made, and unused connections wither and die naturally. And the more we repeat a particular task, the stronger the connections.

1. Experience insulates young neurons with Myelin (white brain matter) so that they are superfast conductors of Electricity.

2. Experienced *synapses* are good at sending electricity to neighbouring neurons (so you're better at lighting up a path you've lit before).

A synapse is the *gap* between one neuron and the next neuron, where the conversation takes place. The electricity in your brain only flows it if reaches the end of a neuron with enough force to jump across that gap.

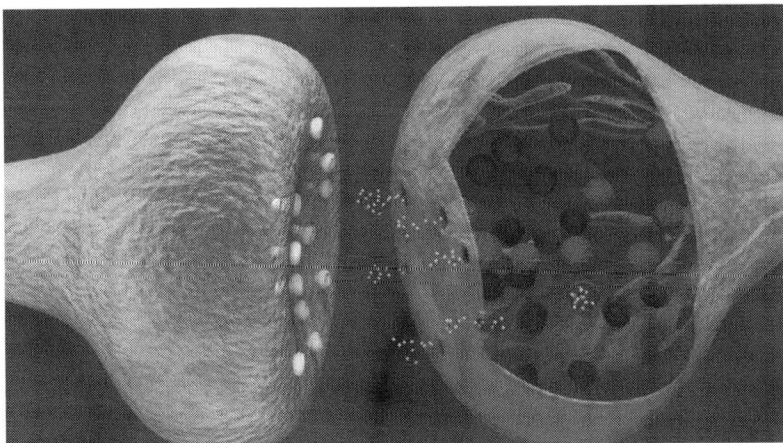

You have around 100 million synapses, and *experience* helps channel your electricity in ways that promote survival - moving away from Pain and towards Pleasure, avoiding Death and increasing your future chances of existing.

Synapse development happens naturally in 2 ways:

(A) REPETITION which develops a synapse *gradually* over time

(B) EMOTION which develops a synapse <u>*INSTANTLY*</u> *(see the NAC technique later on).* Emotions are chemical molecules that can change a synapse *immediately* and *permanently.*

3. Like muscle, neurons *shrink back* if they're not used, so you rely more heavily on the neurons you've used.

4. New synapses grow between the neurons that you use, creating continuous connections.

5. Receptors grow & shrink back, so it's easier to process the feeling that you experience repeatedly.

The brain is in a constant state of learning and adaptive change. See Chapter 23 on NAC for instruction on how to rewire it instantly using *emotion* as the accelerating factor.

Improving PFC Function

Given that the brain is exactly like a muscle – use it or lose it – we can rebuild and strengthen parts of it just by exercising it.

There are two main approaches to improving your Prefrontal Cortex:

1. **Practicing New Behaviours**, in order to build up new circuits and new behaviours *over time*. Strengthen the PFC through continued, repetitive use.

2. **Perform your own Brain Surgery** (just a metaphor, don't worry!) by performing mental exercises (like Mindfulness and NAC) which stimulate your brain to build up new circuits and associated behaviours *rapidly* if powered with enough emotion. You don't just think it, you must FEEL it as well.

* * *

For me personally, I did it the first way by going to Gamblers Anonymous which taught me good habits which I repeated over a sustained period of time. The repetition of these new behaviours reshaped my brain, replacing old moody, reactive, thrill seeking behaviours with better more stable ones that enabled me to build a life and a career. Slow and steady, took years and probably not as exciting, but for me effective and 100% better than the way I lived before.

But ironically at GA I was told *not* look for the reason why I gambled as it wouldn't help me get better. So I didn't look for the answer until I was 25 year clean. And based on my findings, I respectfully disagree. There is a much more efficient way.

On my recovery journey I discovered strategies for improving the mind by studying the works of heroes like Tim Ferris, Gabor Matè, Tony Robbins, Richard Bandler and John Grinder. I have tried to use some of what they taught me to accelerate my own development and help others. Several techniques inspired by them are in this book.

* * *

Summary

1. We discovered that our brain is smarter than any AI computer system on the planet, capable of processing 30 billion bits of information a second and consist of 6,000 miles of wiring, and with a nervous system that consists of 28 billion neurons. And through evolution, it is constantly learning and improving itself all the time.

2. Addiction causes changes to the brain's natural balance, in order to compensate for what you're doing to it.

3. We learned about the 4 main neurotransmitters and how Gamblers generate their own drug-like buzz from them:

   - Serotonin *(reduces anxiety, feeling of calm)*
   - Dopamine *(increases focus, energy and confidence)*
   - Noradrenaline *(increases focus, energy and strength)*
   - Endorphins *(reduces stress, soothes pain)*

4. We looked at how Gamblers regularly get themselves high with these drugs, and how brain patterns are identical to Crack Cocaine and Crystal Meth.

5. We learned that the decision-making part of our brain, the Prefrontal Cortex located in our forehead, actually *shuts down* when we're gambling. This makes it

impossible for us to make the rational decision to stop gambling or walk away until we have no more money or are kicked out.

6. We also learned that any temporary decision-making ability is passed over to our inner "chimp", specifically the *Amygdala* (the centre for Stress, Anxiety, Fear and Memory) and the *Hypothalamus* (the centre for maintaining balance in the brain and body). We also learned how high levels of Stress produces high levels of Cortisol which causes other parts of our brains to shrink and sometimes become incapable of working.

7. We looked briefly the other functions of our (offline) prefrontal cortex, which normally looks after:

    - forming strategies & planning
    - impulse control & delaying gratification
    - considering the future & making predictions
    - foreseeing & weighing possible consequences of behaviour

8. We learned that the Prefrontal Cortex doesn't mature until the age of 25, which explains the reckless behaviour of teenagers. Any repetitive behaviour before this age establishes itself like a "super-circuit" of insulated, highspeed brain neurons. We were also introduced to the concept of ADD (Attention Deficit Disorder) where the prefrontal cortex is already *smaller* and *more underdeveloped* that non-ADD people.

9. We briefly covered Neuroplasticity – the brain's ability to repair and rewire itself (given the correct stimulus).

We noted that there is a slow way and fast way to do this:

- SLOW: Repeating new behaviours which over time develop new synapses (links) between neurons

- FAST: Exercises involving *Emotion* (in real life or in mental visualisation) which develop new synapses *instantly* (see NAC in Chapter 23).

* * *

If you survived this Chapter, very well done! It's not the normal kind of information you expect to find in a Gambling Recovery book, and a lot to take in.

But at least now you know exactly what Gambling is doing to your brain, and continues to do to you each time you gamble.

But I have one more fascinating brain condition to look at, which I suspect you will find equally interesting and may even have.

Chapter 7
The Scattered Mind

Having been in Gamblers Anonymous for 25+ years and prior to that having been a full-on gambling Addict for 10 years, it's probably fair to say that I understand Addiction.

And in those 35 years there's probably not much I haven't seen, heard, experienced, learned or helped pass on to others about Gambling Addiction.

So you can imagine my surprise when just over a year ago – at the age of 52 – I came across a book which made me question everything I thought I knew about Addiction.

As I turned the pages of this book, on practically every page I was saying *"Okay that's me.. yep, that's me again.. me all over.."* literally from start to finish, like someone was playing a joke on me.

Undiagnosed ADD

How did I get to this point? A friend of mine, a Problem Gambler called Tony, told me that he had been to see his GP who told him he had something called *"Undiagnosed*

ADHD". Now I'm no expert but I thought that ADHD was all about hyperactive kids? Tony wasn't hyperactive, just very stressed out (as we all get when we're trying to sort out the chaos we have created and reclaim our lives).

Now I had already listened to an Addiction audiobook called 'In the Realm of the Hungry Ghosts' by Gabor Matè, and in that book he mentioned ADD (*Attention Deficit Disorder* but without the Hyperactive bit).

I had previously tried to read In the Realm but found it heavy going, so listened to the version on Audible instead. I do that often actually - have a book read to me while I read along - as I struggle to keep the focus necessary to read.

Gabor had written a separate smaller book about ADD called "Scattered" so I ordered it. But before I tell you about the book and the link between Gambling Addiction and ADD, let me tell you briefly about the book's author – a most interesting man.

Dr Gabor Matè

Gabor Matè (pronounced Mat-tay) is a General Practitioner who has dedicated large parts of his life to working with Addicts in down-town Vancouver, Canada.

What makes Gabor particularly interesting is the fact that he possesses several Addictive traits of his own, like his

OCD compulsion to buy music CD's. He once spent $8000 in one week on CD's.

Big deal, so he likes his music? Well, most of them remained in their wrappers, unopened. And this man was so compelled by his need to purchase CD's that he would leave whatever he was working on at the time to go buy a CD. And I mean anything. One time he was actually *midway through delivering a baby*, and to the shock of the mother and midwife left to rush off to a CD store! That's compulsion for you, right there.

What's equally interesting is that Gabor has 3 children, all of whom have ADD (diagnosed by independent doctors).

So What IS Attention Deficit Disorder?

ADD is a collection of traits / behaviours, each on its own fairly common but together making up a definite profile or pattern of behaviour. You might think of ADD as the non-Hyperactive version of ADHD, but largely the same.

Dr. Matè describes ADD as a **"brain development disorder"** in which the Prefrontal Cortex – specifically the *Right* Prefrontal Cortex – is underdeveloped, like that of early teenagers. MRI scans have shown that the Prefrontal Cortex in ADD patients is **smaller** than those without ADD. So, they have less decision-making equipment onboard.

ADD patients also have a smaller *Insular* to non-ADD people. The Insular (located in your older "chimp" brain) stores survival-critical information about when your life was in danger, so that you can avoid it in future. It even stores the smells and other aspects of the experience, in order to speed up recall and help us react to it faster.

For instance, you get food poisoning and your Insular stores What, When, Where, When, and How so that in future you avoid that food, that restaurant, and don't put your life in danger again. Or if you have too much of a certain drink and have an extremely bad night, your body recoils at the smell of that drink. Years later even smelling that food or that drink that you were horribly sick on will take you straight back there. That's your Insular doing its job. It plays a key part in telling us to *stay well clear* of something that is harmful to us.

But in ADD people the Insular is less developed, so ADD people have less recall of things that are bad for them.

Typical ADD Traits

Here are some ADD traits and behaviours that I highlighted when reading Scattered. What's particularly interesting is that most of these described me even *before* I first gambled, and describe over 70% of the all Problem Gamblers I have met. With this set of character traits, GA meetings were never boring!

ATTENTION
- Easily distracted
- Becomes distracting or distracted when not the centre of attention
- Tunes out frequently (has heard nothing of what was said).
- Frequent and frustrating memory lapses.
- Poor attention skills (struggles to listen and maintain attention, misses directions)
- Long periods of procrastination (unless mobilised by deadline adrenaline)
- Trouble beginning tasks
- Trouble completing tasks (half-finished books, projects, courses, businesses, DIY)
- Daydreaming (forgetful, jumbled thinking)
- Intensive aversion to boredom
- Misplaces things
- Performs well when given 1-1 attention
- Unproductive when required to work independently

EMOTION
- Emotionally sensitive
- Carries deep emotional hurt (fidgety hands/feet, self-deprecating humour)
- Difficulty relating to siblings
- Abrupt mood changes or temper
- Sometimes anxious under pressure
- Low self esteem
- Class clown, seeks popularity approval
- Joyful events can end in bitter disappointment, sulking, withdrawal
- Trouble maintaining meaningful relationships

PHYSICAL
- Poor Coordination & Clumsiness

IMPULSES	• Impulsive (shopping)
	• Compulsive (OCD, addiction)
TIME	• Usually Late – misjudges how much time required, loses keys, etc
	• Vastly underestimates how long something will take
	• Chronic incapacity to consider the future
OTHER	• Trouble letting go of anything, hoarder
	• Often possesses creative talents that remain unused
	• Described as a person of permanent potential (but never reaching it)

My Own Undiagnosed ADD

Now what interests me is that the above list could have been created from my own end of term school reports, *years before* I was a full-blown gambling addict. As I read 'Scattered' I realised that, like my friend Tony, I also had ADD (whatever that was).

That worried me slightly as I'd never really heard of it, other than something that hyperactive kids apparently have. My teachers had said that I was a little dyslexic at school, and that I just didn't pay attention but had potential. I on the other hand was much more interested in making friends with the people in class and making them laugh (another ADD trait) which was far more interesting to me than looking at a boring blackboard. My need for *Connection* was apparent (a key ADD trait).

Meanwhile my brother was a top student – captain of this sports team and that, achieving straight 'A's at GSCE and A level, then off to read medicine at a top London University. But when people would come to our house they would ask in hushed tones *"And how's Michael getting on?"* to which the reply was always an embarrassed *"I'm sure he'll find something that he enjoys…"*

At 17 my Dad sent me off to a career assessment day comprising of IQ tests and psychological interviews for which he paid a lot of money. The results that came back said: *"He can do whatever he sets his mind to"* which my father was a little putout about, as he had paid handsomely to be told the obvious.

But ironically I find out years later that a key ADD trait is that you *cannot* simply "set your mind on something" without someone actively helping you. When asked to focus, an ADD person's attention flies off in different directions, and brain wave activity actually *decreases* as their brain switches off rather than switch on. This explains why I couldn't learn at school and struggled later on when I taught myself IT and programming after my gambling days. I had to read each book x6 times each, and they were big books that looked more like Simplified Chinese to me. But I kept telling myself that if I knew what was in the pages then I could make a living.

> *However the real magic moment for me came when I realised only recently – a quarter of a century after I last gambled - that I wasn't primary addicted to Gambling,* **I was addicted to being woken up and engaged by the machines.**
>
> *When in action my ADD brain was fully stimulated and fully engaged. I felt normal, capable, focussed (until the shutdown phase at least).*

ADD is the missing piece of the puzzle for me. And if tomorrow they turn around and say there are 600,000 people in the UK with a gambling problem and what a coincidence there are also 600,000 people with undiagnosed ADD, it would be no surprise to me.

I have personally talked with a LOT of gamblers over the years and most of them fit the profile in my view. I think I'm right that Gabor Matè says at least 70% of the addiction clients that he saw over 10 years all had ADD in his view. For me it's a lot higher.

Gambling and ADD

Here are some selected excerpts taken from Chapter 30 of 'Scattered' (the chapter specifically on Addiction) which illustrate Gabor's superior understanding of the subject.

But I highly recommend you get your own copy of Scattered as I have barely touched the surface (get it <u>here</u>).

"All addictions are anaesthetics.

They separate us from the distress of our consciousness. We throw off our familiar and tired consciousness to assume another mind state we find more comfortable, at least temporarily.

Desperate to be out of our mind and unaware, we surrender to the addiction, to be lulled into a walking sleep."

"I could not have been more focused when in engaged in my addiction. My brain was fully alert. My pre-frontal lobes were awash with Endorphins and Dopamine, realise by the thrill of the hunt and acquisition.

The addiction, in a strange way, makes the addict feel more connected to life. The downside is that it separates him further and further from himself.

He is feeding only his appetite, not his hunger."

"In biochemical terms, any addictive substance or behaviour is self-medication, self-administered emotional pain relief.

But the ADD person is also treating herself for a condition she is not even aware of having."

"Less obvious but no less physiological are the effects on the brain of self-stimulating behaviours.

The gambler and the sexaholic, the compulsive shopper and the man or woman who insist on skiing uncharted glaciers are all looking for the same hit of Dopamine and Endorphins that the ingestion of substances get the drug addict. Whatever gets you through the night. Those of us with Attention Deficit Disorder *love* Dopamine and Endorphins."

What are the Causes of ADD?

At its core, ADD behaviour is the result of an immature brain that failed to complete its journey to maturity. What should have been a normal **Stage** in childhood and outgrown/overwritten, becomes a **STATE** that is repeatedly exhibited throughout adulthood.

As Gabor Matè observes: *"We are born with no capacity whatsoever to set-regulate emotion or action. For self-regulation to be possible, specifically brain centres have to develop and grow connections with other important nerve centres, and chemical pathways have to be established."*

"ADD is a prime illustration of how the adult continues to struggle with the unsolved problems of childhood. She is held back precisely at the point where the child did not develop, hampered in those areas where the infant or toddler got stuck during the course of development."

As Gabor himself says, the ADD brain is caused by Genes and Parenting (but not necessarily *bad* genes and *bad* parenting).

Adverse Childhood Experiences (ACE) also appear to influence ADD. I don't intend to cover it in detail in this book, but there is a strong link between childhood trauma and various addictions. I myself was sent off to a boarding school with the promise of a great education. Between the daily physical beatings and the mental bullying, you could say I got an 'education'... or rather PTSD. I used to be allowed home occasionally on a Sunday and would spend all day in my room crying, dreading going back that night. But with what I know now, I was a sensitive child that was already a little ADD when I got to that school. And the PTSD trauma I experienced there would have further stunted my brain's development from reaching full maturity. I didn't realise it for 40 years.

PTSD (Post Traumatic Stress Disorder)

According to a report (Feb 2019) in the Lancet, 7.8% of all children now have PTSD due to *bullying* & *violence*. To the subconscious mind that has little understanding of time, some of these patterns are still running in the background as if they happened yesterday, even though it has been years. It is no wonder that the number of problem gamblers looking to self-medicate is on the rise (see blog for details).

Parents and ADD

I approach this section with extreme caution. No-one is blaming the parents, certainly not me. But so much of an infant's world is shaped by her parents, or rather her *perception* of her parents and her *perception* of their love for her. The love that we give is not always the love that is received.

Within minutes of a baby being born, the mother's odour stimulates the branching of millions of nerve cells in the newborn's brain. A 6-day old baby can already distinguish her mother from other mothers by smell. [Note that the 'mother' here of course is the primary care giver which might also be a grandparent, father, or non-biological carer.]

Between 2-7 weeks the infant's right brain will develop by watching the mother's right brain through her gaze and tone. The baby naturally looks away first because she becomes overstimulated by the experience. She might first experience *shame* when her mother does not hold her gaze or looks away first. If the mother or primary caregiver looks away first, the sensitive baby interprets this being as being ignored and as not being good enough to be loved. If this becomes a routine, the infant's brain will begin to develop differently to another infant whose mother did not look away first, and we have started on the path to ADD with a less developed Prefrontal Cortex and less opioid pleasure receptors.

Later at school the ADD child will look to make connections with her peers in the classroom, as her need for *Connection* is more important to her than her need for learning. She will spend much of her life looking for connection, for approval, which she feels she did not get when she was young.

In babies a major part of this bonding process is *Attunement*, where the baby learns to trust the primary caregiver. They build a bond whereby the infant leads, and the caregiver mirrors and follows. In this phase the baby can see, sense and feel emotion, all which contribute to the infant's learning and brain development. So things like post-natal depression can have an ADD effect. Attunement goes on to become the foundation for Attachment, our need to be close to somebody which is essential for human survival.

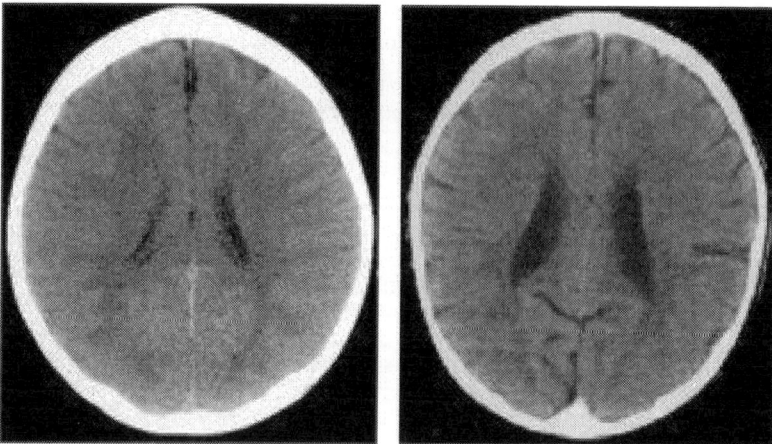

Dark undeveloped parts of a 3yr old brain caused by attunement / attachment disorder

"Humans, from the instant of birth, require a constant stream of emotional, spiritual, psychological, and physical inputs from another loving human", says Dr. Mary Jo Barrett of the University of Chicago — *"just as we require air, food, and liquid"*.

Similarly throughout childhood, the nurturing bond between child and parent (specifically the primary caregiver) should not be broken.

But modern life is busy. Children are put into nursery while the parents are out earning the money, divorces are frequent, stress and anxiety from social media is high, and so on.

As our kids grow, we provide them with the latest gadgets to babysit them, forgetting that keeping them entertained is very different from *interacting* with them. Children are being educated by games, Netflix and social media, and their brains are developing (or not developing) accordingly. I would expect to see ADD rates triple in the next 5 years, and with it the number of Addicts looking for *"the warm hug of a mother"* as Gabor Matè puts it.

Due to war, Gabor's mother was separated from her newborn for 3 months, which to a new brain would have been interpreted as abandonment. His mother loved him dearly, but the child had no way of knowing this. Abandonment, or rather *perceived* abandonment, resulted in ADD.

My own mother was always there, but also not there. She was physically present, saying and doing all the right things, yet I can count on the fingers of one hand the times we really connected as Mother and Son. I remember as an infant being directed to sit and play with toys while (from my perception) she doted on my brother. She was more like a school teacher than a mother, bless her. *Yet I know that she loved me and gave me all the love she had to give.* Perhaps the ADD predisposition (possibility of developing it) was genetically passed down, who knows. Certainly there was addiction further up my family tree.

But blaming the past is not a strategy for building the future. If there IS any underdevelopment in our brains due to ADD or childhood Trauma (or both) then it is my view that we can take responsibility as adults to strengthen what is weak using the exercises in this book. Having a victim mentality will not help us strengthen what is weak and build up.

My Children and ADD

Gabor Matè has four children, three of which have been diagnosed with ADD by independent practitioners.

As a father myself of two teenagers I can now see that one clearly has ADD and one does not. The girl (a female carbon copy of me) exhibits all the typical traits – putting things off, not paying attention at school, highly sociable, easily distracted, creative, sensitive, etc.

You can give both children the same task and:

- One listens, does it exactly like you've asked him to, and gets on with it with single-minded focus (just like my own brother did)
- The other doesn't listen, gets distracted, wonders why she has to do it in the first place, and her mind fires of in 5 different directions at once like a firework display! Then she puts it off for ever and finally stays up all night trying to get it done last minute. She is her father's daughter.

Is it genetic? I don't know, maybe. It's most probably a genetic *disposition* that is passed down, that may or may not happen dependent on circumstances and environment.

Was it caused by me being largely absent and focussing on my work when she was a baby? I don't know, maybe. ADD is caused in babies by the parents physically not being there, or physically there but perceived as emotionally distant. The sensitive infant doesn't distinguish between the two - absent is absent.

Either way, we discuss and laugh about it now. We compare our funny habits and the conversation is always full of *"No way, I do that!"* type banter. I coach her through it, showing how ADD can be a massive strength if recognised and utilised in the right way. A lot of the larger-than-life characters in this world are clearly ADD. And each new time she handles it, her brain naturally builds the underlying neuron infrastructure that it needs to function more efficiently next time.

What does an ADD brain look like?

Much of ADD behaviour is governed by what goes on in the *right prefrontal cortex* (PFC), an area of the brain just behind the forehead over the eye sockets. Remember the PFC from the previous chapter on Dopamine and other Neurotransmitters? Here it is again.

The word *Cortex* incidentally means 'bark' (as in the bark of a tree) and refers to the thin rim of grey matter covering the white matter of the brain. Spread out it would be about the size and thickness of a table napkin.

The prefrontal cortex basically governs impulsive control, social-emotional intelligence, and motivation. As we saw earlier, it is the Executive **Decision-Making Centre** of the brain.

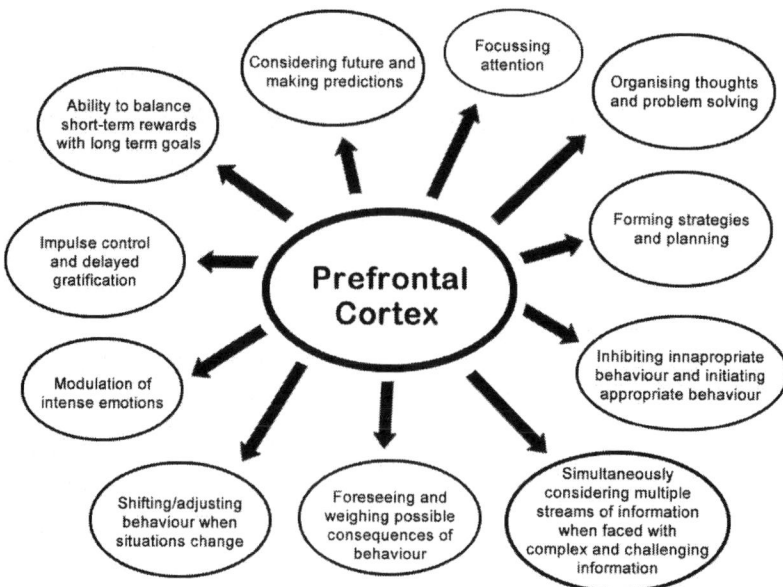

People that have received injuries to the forehead area soon start to exhibit classic ADD behaviours, like distractibility and poor regulation of impulses. Monkeys and lab rats that have been subjected to prefrontal interference soon lose the ability to read social cues and participate in socially essential activities, such as mutual grooming. Not long after they are ostracised by other members of the group, as their Connection with the group has been diminished.

MRI scans of ADD patients have shown the prefrontal cortex to be physically *smaller* than non-ADD patients. And when examined by EEG (which measure the brain's electrical wave activity) a normal brain would speed UP during reading and drawing tasks (as expected) whereas the ADD brain would actually **slow down** making it harder for them to get started on things.

As such, people with ADD can have poor internal supervision, short attention span, distractibility, disorganisation, and hyperactivity (although only half the people with ADD are hyperactive), impulse control problems, difficulty learning from past errors, lack of forethought, and procrastination. I personally tick most of those boxes.

The more people with ADD try to concentrate, the worse things get for them. Instead of increasing as it should, the activity in the PFC will actually decrease causing them to tune out, get distracted, and take longer to complete tasks. I wonder if teachers know how to spot ADD? Mine certainly didn't.

The Sleeping Policeman

Gabor Matè thinks of the prefrontal cortex as a 'policeman' whose main role is to make sense of thoughts, sensations and impulses coming into it from the lower brain centres. The prefrontal cortex must then select what is useful and helpful, and block out what is not useful to the current situation or our survival in any given situation.

The cortex has a split second to make this unconscious choice: **to allow the impulse or to cancel it.**

This explains why a Problem Gambler acts out on the urge to bet again, as the Policeman whose job it was to wave the danger flag was asleep on duty.

This is shocking. A Gambling Addict in the middle of a session is literally be *unable to decide to walk away* from the machine or call it a day.

Zombie-like they go through the motions, waiting to be woken up again when it's over - exhausted and a LOT poorer.

Treatment for ADD

ADD is treated with stimulants, the main objective being to wake up the prefrontal cortex, the sleeping policeman.

One such treatment is Ritalin (Methylphenidate HCL) which is used to increase attention and decrease impulsiveness and hyperactivity. Patients who take Ritalin often describe the 'fog' lifting within 20-30 minutes and being able to think clearly for the first time in their life.

Ritalin and other psychostimulants are thought to increase the availability of Dopamine in the brain's prefrontal areas, which in turn is supposed to increase motivation and attention by improving the function of the PFC. However many think this is too simple an explanation as it does not take into account the balance of the other Neurotransmitters like Serotonin.

Undiagnosed ADD addicts (like me and maybe you) are probably already turning to non-medical stimulants to wake ourselves up:

- Gambling
- Drugs
- Alcohol
- Nicotine
- Caffeine
- Porn
- Chocolate/Sugar
- Dangerous Driving/Pursuits

It is only when we are getting a significant stimulant that our prefrontal cortex wakes up and starts doing its job. This is why Addicts often describe themselves as feeling fantastic when doing their drug of choice, despite the fact that it is ruining their life.

I remember my early days in GA when people would rush out in the break to light up outside and puff furiously on their cigarettes to get a nicotine hit. I was one of them for the first year.

Many of these other stimulants go on to become Addictions in their own right, and many people turned up at meetings with dual addictions for the same underlying problem. *One problem, different attempts to solve it.*

They didn't realise it at the time, but these other stimulants were simply different approaches to try and wake up their Prefrontal Cortex, their Sleeping Policeman.

Is Ritalin a Cure for Gambling?

A word of caution before you start thinking that an NHS prescribed stimulant is the cure for Problem gambling. A stimulant might induce clarity, but I doubt it will help address the Gambling Addiction which your brain has become hardwired to engage in over hundreds or thousands of hours of gambling behaviour.

As someone once said: *"Neurons that fire together, wire together"* and your brain contains a super circuit of gambling wiring! Even if a stimulant helps you to think more clearly, the underlying gambling pattern will still need to be addressed.

I personally don't intend to try it as I address my ADD from the mental perspective, helping my teenage brain develop into an adult one. But don't let me put you off talking to your doctor about it.

Just be mindful of the fact that if your life is messy (and it most likely is) do you really want to see it with more clarity right now? Or would you rather just get on with putting new practices and behaviours in place that help the mind naturally repair & stimulate itself.

* * *

Summary

1. I introduced you to the most interesting Dr Gabor Matè (an addiction doctor and addict himself) and his ground-breaking work in the field of addiction (author of "Scattered"). He was one of the first to establish a link between Attention Deficit Disorder and Addiction and deserves all the credit – you may have noticed they even share the first three same letters: **ADDiction.**

2. We learned that ADD is a brain development disorder of the right prefrontal cortex, which is physically smaller in people with ADD. The Insular, the area which helps us remember and avoid adverse situations, is also smaller.

3. We looked at a list of ADD traits that affect Attention, Emotion, the Physical body, Impulses, Time, and a few other things. I personally ticked a lot of those boxes, which was a surprise as I am 53 years old and had never heard of ADD! But it makes me feel better to know that Gabor also didn't discover his ADD until middle age.

4. We considered the possible causes of ADD, from a genetic likelihood, to Adverse Childhood Experiences (resulting in PTSD) to our parents who may have been physically or emotionally absent. But the love given is not always the love received, and they gave us all the love they had to give. As adults we can now take

responsibly for any brain underdevelopment and regrow what is missing using the techniques in this book.

5. We found out that not only is the prefrontal cortex in ADD people smaller than normal, but the ADD brain actually *slows down* when asked to concentrate on a task rather than speed up as we would expect.

6. We looked again at how our decision-making prefrontal cortex falls asleep on the job (Sleeping Policeman) and how we are basically zombie-like, in a trance in front of a screen or machine for this very reason.

7. Stimulants are the treatment for ADD and we covered some typical ways that Undiagnosed ADD people already stimulate themselves, and then looked briefly at a commonly prescribed treatment, Ritalin. My own thoughts are that Ritalin may well give immediate clarity of thought, but we still have the addiction and the underlying wiring to address, as well as the underlying problem which we seek to escape or avoid.

A
CONNECTION
DISORDER

Chapter 8

Rat Park

Let's leave Gambling for a while to examine Drug Addiction, and see what can be learned.

In 1978, Canadian psychologist Bruce K. Alexander conducted an experiment that would revolutionise the way we understand drug addiction. Alexander and his colleagues built a large colony to house rats, with more than 200 times the floor space of a standard lab rat cage. This Rat Park experiment culminated in the leading breakthrough of the time: *the underlying connection between a person's environment and addiction.*

The Rat Park Experiment aimed to prove that Psychology – a person's mental, emotional, and psychosocial states – was the greatest cause of Addiction, not the drug itself. Prior to Alexander's experiment, addiction studies using lab rats did not alter the rat's environment. Scientists placed rats in tiny, isolated cages and starved them for hours on end. The Skinner Boxes the rats lived in 24x7 allowed no room for movement and no interaction with other rats, a bit like a solitary prison cell.

Using the boxes, scientists hooked rats up to various drugs using intravenous needles implanted in their jugular veins. The rats could then choose to inject themselves with the drug by pushing a lever in the cage.

Scientists studied drug addiction this way, testing with Heroin, Amphetamine, Morphine, and Cocaine. Typically, the rats would press the lever often enough to consume large doses of the drugs. The studies naturally concluded that the drugs were irresistibly addictive by their specific properties.

Solitary Confinement

However, rats by nature are social, industrious creatures that thrive on contact and communication with other rats. Putting a rat in solitary confinement does the same thing as to a human - it drives them insane. If prisoners in solitary confinement had the option to take mind-numbing narcotics, they most likely would.

The Skinner Box studies also made it incredibly easy for rats to take the drugs, and it offered no alternatives. The need for a different type of study was clear - enter Bruce K. Alexander.

Rat Park Study

The goal of Alexander's experiment was to prove that drugs do not cause addiction, but that *living conditions* do. He wanted to refute other studies that connected opiate addiction in laboratory rats to addictive properties within the drug itself.

So rather than the small, bare, confined Skinner boxes Alexander built the equivalent of a Rat Theme Park. A big enclosure made out of plywood, some *x200 times bigger* than the tiny cages, with painted walls containing woodland scenes. They covered the floor with fragrant cedar shavings for the rats to nest in, and scattered cans for the rats to hide and play in.

There were wheels and balls for play, plenty of food, 16-20 rats of both sexes mingling with one another, and plenty of mating space. Everything that a happy rat could possibly want to enjoy themselves.

Drug Solution or Plain Water

Alexander tested a variety of theories using different experiments with Rat Park, to show that the rat's environment played the largest part in whether a rat became addicted to drugs or not.

In the experiment, the social rats had the choice to drink fluids from one of two dispensers. One had plain tap water, and the other had a morphine solution. The scientists ran a variety of experiments to test the rats' willingness to consume the morphine solution compared to rats in solitary confinement.

The Seduction Experiment

32 rats (16 male & 16 female) were randomly assigned isolated cages.

Day 1-3	The rats were given a choice of two liquids (one sugary syrup and one bitter quinine) and their intake of each was measured. Neither of the solutions contained drugs.	RESULT: The team learned that both groups of rats loved the sugary solution and hated the bitter one.

Day 4-8	The rats were also tested with a non-drugged combination solution containing both the bitter quinine and the sweet sugar.	
Day 9-13	They tried to seduce the rats into drinking a morphine solution (similar to Heroin) by gradually adding sugar to make it sweet.	The rats avoided the bitter drug water at first, but as the solution got sweeter so did the rats consumption of it, and in higher volumes. The consumption by the rats in the isolated cages was x19 times higher than Rat Park at certain dosages. They started on it earlier too in order to relieve their distress.
Day 14-19		Caged rats would drift off into a drugged haze, but the rats in the Park largely left the freely-available morphine solution.

Day 19-23	More sugar was introduced	The caged rats consumed more and were out of it most of the time, whereas the rats in the Park continued to avoid it.
Day 24-28	Finally the researchers mixed up an irresistible sugary cocktail solution with just a small amount of drugs	The rats in the Park which had avoided the heavy drug solution began drinking the lightly drugged cocktail syrup.

Drug Rat Rehab

In another Rat Park Experiment, Alexander took 32 new rats and got them completed addicted, then placed 10 of them in the isolation cages and 22 in the Park. He then introduced intermittent "Choice" days where the rats could choose from plain water or the morphine water.

The results were in keeping with the findings so far. The caged rats kept choosing the drug to get them through, whereas the rats in the Park decreased their intake by choosing water on Choice days, gradually weaning themselves off. Yes, they exhibited the typical twitchy withdrawal symptoms, but chose to go through it in order to return to their normal social life.

In yet another test, caged rats that were fed nothing but morphine water for 57 days chose the plain water when moved into Rat Park, voluntarily going through withdrawal!

The rats in the larger, free range enclosure consistently resisted the morphine water, preferring plain water instead (and their social life).

No matter what they tried, Alexander and his team couldn't get the rats in the Park to take the drugged water! They even tried adding large quantities of sugar but still the rats left it, choosing the plain water instead. The only time they went for it was when it was a mild solution mixed in with a truly irresistible cocktail. And even then they only had it in small amounts.

Lessons from Rat Park

Based on the study, the team concluded that drugs themselves *do not* cause addictions. Rather, a *person's environment* feeds an Addiction. Feelings of isolation, loneliness, hopelessness, and lack of control based on unsatisfactory living conditions make a person dependent on substances. Under normal living conditions, people can resist drug addiction and generally prefer reality altogether.

What scientists today realise is that addiction is as mental as it is physical. Humans do not have to be physically isolated, like the rats in the Skinner Boxes, to become addicted to substances. Emotional isolation is enough to produce the same affects. Humans cope with their feelings of dislocation with Gambling, Drugs and Alcohol, finding an escape or a way to numb the pain. A human's cage may be invisible, but it is no less there.

The learning from this is clear: Addiction is largely *psychological*, even with substances like drugs and alcohol. A holistic approach is needed, addressing a person's mental, emotional, social, and spiritual needs, and reconnecting them to others.

Alexander himself draws some very interesting conclusions on Society and how it helps *create* addicts:

> "When I talk to addicted people, whether they are addicted to alcohol, drugs, gambling, internet use, sex, or anything

else, I encounter human beings who really do not have a viable social or cultural life. **They use their addictions as a way of coping with their dislocation: as an escape, a pain killer, or a kind of substitute for a full life.** More and more psychologists and psychiatrists are reporting similar observations. Maybe our fragmented, mobile, ever-changing modern society has produced social and cultural isolation in very large numbers of people, even though their cages are invisible!

The view of addiction from Rat Park is that **today's flood of addiction is occurring because our hyperindividualistic, hypercompetitive, frantic, crisis-ridden society makes most people feel social and culturally isolated.** Chronic isolation causes people to look for relief. They find temporary relief in addiction to drugs or any of a thousand other habits and pursuits because addiction allows them to escape from their feelings, to deaden their senses, and to experience an addictive lifestyle as a substitute for a full life."

Bruce K. Alexander

* * *

SUMMARY

People, like rats, are social animals. But isolate them and they experience unbearable emotional pain which they will do anything to self-medicate themselves from, in order to reduce the stress.

QUESTION: What might YOU be disconnected from?

Chapter 9
Vietnam

In 1971, as the Vietnam War entered its sixteenth year, the US government discovered that over 15% of the 3 million US soldiers stationed out there were Heroin addicts. Follow up research revealed that 35% of service members had tried Heroin and as many as 20% were addicted.

Soldiers would regularly see their friends killed and be called upon to kill men, women and children in a never-ending nightmare. Many of their friends were doing heroin and they were thousands of miles from home. Given the horrors these young men had to endure, it was not surprising that they couldn't bear to be present in themselves.

Heroin use (escape) was their *response* to the disconnection and dislocation with their families, to get *temporary relief* from the problem.

Spontaneous Remission

At the time Heroin Addiction was considered to be a permanent and irreversible condition. But Lee Robins, one of the researchers in charge, made a major and very unusual discovery.

He found that 9 out 10 of the soldiers automatically & spontaneously *gave up* their heroin addiction on returning home and being reconnected with their loved ones.

Furthermore only 5% of them became re-addicted within a year, and just 12% relapsed within 3 years.

These facts were in stark contrast to the heroin rehab statistics in the US at the time, where 90% of heroin users would become re-addicted once they returned to their home environment from rehab.

Could Connection be the Cure?

Just like the rats in Rat Park, nearly all of the soldiers returning from Vietnam simply no longer needed their heroin addiction anymore and discarded it, often with the minimal of withdrawal symptoms.

Addiction served a *purpose*, which in the case of the soldiers was to help them forget the horrors of war, helping them not be present in themselves. The rats in the isolation cages did the same thing.

Yet when their environment included love, connection with others, support, and enjoyment they no longer felt the need to escape themselves. They chose life instead.

* * *

SUMMARY

Heroin Addiction was thought to be permanent and one of the hardest things to escape. Yet when reconnected with their lives and their loved ones, nearly all the returning soldiers spontaneously gave up Heroin, and most stayed off too.

> **QUESTION:** What purpose is YOUR addiction serving? What's it helping *you* escape from, avoid, or get through?

Chapter 10
The Six Human Needs

It is widely accepted that every human being on the planet has Six Human Needs, as per the psychological model developed by Anthony Robbins and Cloe Madanes.

The first four are the needs of the *Personality* and help us to Live, to function. We will meet them one way or another (in a good way or an unhealthy way).

	Description	*Words Used*
CERTAINTY	The need for security, comfort and consistency.	Comfort, stability, feeling grounded, predictability, protection, consistency
UNCERTAINTY / VARIETY	The need for variety, to have challenges that exercise your physical and emotion range (and break up the boredom of certainly!)	Fear, instability, change, chaos, entertainment, suspense, surprise, conflict, crisis
SIGNIFICANCE	The need to feel important, needed, wanted and worthy of love. To feel a sense of	Pride, importance, standards, achievement,

	being important is necessary to all human beings.	performance, competition
LOVE */* **CONNECTION**	The need for the experience of Love and Connection. Everyone needs to connect with other human beings and strives/hopes for LOVE (but will settle for CONNECTION).	Togetherness, passion, unity, warmth, tenderness, desire

The last two are the needs of the *Soul* and help us to Thrive, make us feel **Fulfilled**.

GROWTH	As humans we need to constantly develop emotionally, intellectually, and spiritually. Some people by working out physically, by reading books, or by helping others. When we stop growing, we die. Staying still is not enough. Anything that you want to remain in your life (health, relationship, happiness, love, money) must be cultivated and expanded with growth.	Reading, working out, learning, developing

| CONTRIBUTION | As humans we need to go beyond our own needs and give to others. A life is incomplete without the sense the one is making a contribution to others or to a cause.

Incidentally *Contribution* is a sure way to ensure the other needs are met too (as Contributing usually provides challenges, love/connection, significance and certainty). | Community service, writing a book, volunteering, supporting others with their addiction |
| --- | --- | --- |

Addiction

When ONE specific object, activity or substance meets THREE out of the first four needs, it's an **Addiction**.

Certainty	Feeling Secure
Uncertainty / Variety	Feeling challenged
Significance	Feeling recognised / important
Love / Connection	Feeling connected and nurtured
Growth	Constantly developing
Contribution	Giving to others

Could this be True for our Gambling Addiction?

For example, I might get the Certainty/consistency from playing the same game, the Variety and thrill of not knowing if I will win and throwing it all to the wind, and the Significance from the occasional win. If this is the case then gambling has just pushed all my buttons, and the Addiction is embedded in my psychology as something that is important to my survival. Hold that thought.

As for Growth and Contribution, most gamblers don't even get started on meeting these needs as they are still struggling with the first 4 needs (usually meeting them in unhealthy ways).

Meeting Other People's Needs

Gambling Addiction is a totally selfish activity which some would classify as **Immature**. Part of our recovery is thinking about others, specifically how we meet *their* needs.

This might be your partner, your children, etc.

- If you satisfy TWO of someone else's needs, you have a *connection.*

- If you satisfy FOUR of someone else's needs, you have a *strong attachment.*

- If you satisfy SIX of someone else's needs, the person is *permanently bonded* to you.

Gambling is a selfish addiction where we are totally and constantly consumed with ourselves. A good starting point to recovering your own personality (and therefore your underlying brain function) is to start trying to meet the needs of the others in any ways you can, big or small.

The Need for Connection

In the previous chapters we learned about *Connection* being the missing link for the Rats in the isolated cages and the Soldiers far away from home in Vietnam, and how both dropped their addictions fairly automatically and painlessly upon reconnection to their friends and family.

And back in the ADD section we saw how a break in Connection with the mother or even a *perceived* break of that Connection resulted in a decrease in the brain's development, specifically in the Right Prefrontal Cortex.

So it's interesting to see **Connection** appearing again, this time as one of the primary needs of the Personality. As we saw earlier:

> If any ONE thing
>
> meets **THREE** of our first FOUR needs
>
> it's an ***Addiction.***

Could it therefore be that we are using Gambling to meet our need for Connection? Replacing genuine love and affection with a screen or a machine? Establishing a bond with something artificial doesn't love us back? Substituting real life family and friends for something we can control? No wonder our life is falling apart.

Substitute Connection

Let me share a personal story with you to illustrate how this works. I started Gambling compulsively when I was 18 at University. Four months earlier I had split up from a girl that I was very much in love with. When she dumped me I was devastated, completely heartbroken.

Three things happened which are relevant:

(1) When she dumped me I started putting neat Rum in my coffee and drinking it in the mornings. It took the edge off the emotional hurt and helped me to get through the day. I did not want pain like that in my mind and my body, as I felt like I couldn't handle it.

(2) Just before going to University I started seeing someone new who smoked. Despite being healthy and a proud non-smoker, I picked up her cigarettes and smoked them until I nearly made myself sick. I then smoked 20 a day for the next ten years. When I first started smoking, I remember thinking immature thoughts like *"What's the point?"* and feeling generally worthless, like it didn't matter if I hurt myself.

(3) Six weeks later I was walking past a machine in the Student Union when someone asked me for money. Suddenly it dropped the Jackpot and I experienced extreme SIGNIFICANCE when everyone wanted to know who go "it". All feelings of not being good enough vanished INSTANTLY. In that moment I was successful, I was enough – just like I felt when I was

with my ex-girlfriend before she broke my heart. This machine had given me temporary relief from those feelings, and made me feel FANTASTIC. Me and my friends went to the bar and had free drinks all afternoon – my social CONNECTION was maxed out. Life didn't get much better than that.

I didn't realise it at the time, but I had replaced my Ex with a Connection to a machine. Gambling now gave me all the same feelings I used to get when I was with her - that feeling of being enough, loved, special, on top of the world. I had started a relationship with Gambling - bonding with a brightly-lit, glass-fronted machine that spoke to me in encouraging and sometimes congratulating tones. It told me a few times that I was the best, a winner, and many more times that I was SO CLOSE to being great if I could only just try harder, spend a little longer, have just one more attempt to win its approval. And the vulnerable, off-balance me, believed it.

Over the next few weeks I also didn't realise that Gambling had now begun to meet at least THREE of my first Four needs:

Certainty – I would always get that feeling of excitement, anticipation

Variety – There was a challenge and I didn't know if I would win

Connection – I felt connected, alive, engaged

136

Significance – I felt significant, especially when I won. People used to watch me play the machines like I had some kind of skill.

* * *

SUMMARY

Everyone meets the first four human needs one way or another, and as Gamblers we hardly ever meet the last two.

I know from my own experience how Gambling met several of my needs – or rather how I *used* Gambling to meet several of my needs, rather than making healthier choices.

QUESTION

How are you meeting YOUR first Four needs?

Are you meeting the last two (Growth and Contribution) in any way at all?

Can you remember the last time you did?

Summary

1. We looked at the work of Bruce Alexander in the 1970's and his "Rat Park" experiments where he compared isolated rats with happy, free range rats. Interestingly the happy, stress free rats with opportunities to socialise would nearly always choose plain water, whereas the rats with stress always chose the drugged water to self-medicate their mental anguish and escape their isolation.

2. Alexander performed many types of experiment, taking them from one environment to other and the results were always the same. His conclusion was that addiction is not caused by a substance or behaviour, but solely by the subject's environment. He deduced that Addiction is a response to isolation and pain, and that Addiction is a choice: a self-medicating coping mechanism, to help us escape ourselves.

3. We switched to look at the Vietnam War and how 20% of the 3 million soldiers were addicted to heroin to get them through the horrors of war, and the emotional distress of being away from their families on the other side of the world.

4. We noted how 90% of them spontaneously gave up their heroin addiction on returning to the United States and being reunited with their families. And only 5% of the veterans became readdicted to heroin within the

next 12 months, in stark contrast to the 90% of heroin addicts coming out of traditional rehab. Just like the rats in the park, if we are located in a safe and social environment where we are connected to those we love and who love us, then there is far less need to escape ourselves or self-medicate.

5. We then looked at the Six Humans Needs, the first four which are the needs of the Personality. We will meet these first four in healthy ways or unhealthy ways. We noted that when *one* thing meets any THREE or more of the first four needs, then it's an Addiction (like it did with myself).

Certainty	Feeling Secure
Uncertainty / Variety	Feeling challenged
Significance	Feeling recognised / important
Love / Connection	Feeling connected and nurtured
Growth	Constantly developing
Contribution	Giving to others

6. We looked briefly at the last two needs, *Growth* and *Contribution*, which make us feel fulfilled. As gamblers we rarely experience much of these two.

7. We noted CONNECTION coming up again, just like in Rat Park and Vietnam, and previously in ADD as well – a recurring theme. Clearly connection is part of the solution, and probably also Growth and Contribution, all which are all qualities of a maturing mind.

8. Finally we gave some consideration to how we can try to meet the Six Human Needs of those closest to us.

139

PREPARING
TO
REPAIR

Chapter 11
Reality Check

Before we make a start, let's establish some basics. The purpose of this is to work out for real how much time and money you've spent on gambling, and a few other things. No more sticking our heads in the sand – we're going to allow our brain to see we've been deceiving it.

So take a deep breath, get a pen & paper, and a get a calculator up on your device. We're about to look at our gambling from a whole new perspective: The Truth.

#1 - Work out your **Numbers**

Firstly write down roughly how many hours a day you would spend gambling. 1 hour, 2 hours, 3 hours? Whatever that average number normally would be. Obviously you might gamble more or perhaps less on weekends, so take that into account when working out your average daily number. This is time actually spent in front of a machine, at a casino, or in front of screen gambling. BE HONEST.

Then work out how many hours total by using this method:

Average Hours per Day x Weeks per Year x No of Years

Hours per Day: Give an average
Hours per Week: Times your Hours per Day by 6
Hours per Year: Times your Hours per Week by 50

Total: Times your Hours per Year by No of Years

Example: If I gamble on average 2 hours a day, most days of the week and for most of the year, and have been gambling for say 3 years, then my calculation is:

2 x 6 days = 12 Hours per **Week**
12 x 50 weeks = 600 Hours per **Year**
600 x 3 years = **1,800 Hours Total**

MY TIME: _____

OK now we've got our TIME. Stop looking at it, thinking *"that can't be right"*.

Now we're going to use the same principle to work out how much MONEY we spend on gambling.

> *Example:* If I get through an average of £100 a day on gambling, roughly 6 days a week for most of the year, and gambling like this for 5 years, then my calculation is:
>
> £100 x 6 = £600 per **Week**
> £600 x 50 = £30,000 per **Year**
> £30k x 5 = **£150,000 Total**

MY MONEY: _____

How much did that come to? You're brain's thinking *"No way, that's not right!"* It does this because you have what Psychologists call a **Cognitive Distortion**, a blind spot, where your brain HAS to fool you in order to let you do it in the first place.

You see you've been gambling to win money, a jackpot for example, but don't realise that you've spent many, many times MORE than that trying to win that money.

The reason we're working this out now is to give ourselves *leverage*, as there's some hard work ahead. Look at those numbers – they are YOUR numbers. Allow yourself to feel something about those numbers and strengthen your resolve to do whatever it takes to sort this once and for all.

Think about what your annual salary is and how hard you had to work to earn it. What would it be like if someone gave you a cheque for this number right now? Feel your responses.

#2 - Understand **the Price** you've Paid

Next we're going to work out what gambling has already cost us. Obviously a key element of this will be money (in terms of our total debts) but we're also going to note the *other* things that gambling has cost us like relationships, opportunities, jobs, houses, health, etc. Again make a list and BE HONEST.

Also write down the total amount you owe (secured and unsecured loans, cards, personal debts, everything). BE HONEST. We owe that whether we care to admit it or not, so we need to at least have some idea of the figure.

Don't be overly worried by this step. Even if you owe a very large amount of money (say £200,000) you might earn 3-5 times that in the course of your working life. We'll get into practical solutions later on.

#3 - Know your **Why**

Now write down your WHY. *Why* you want to give up gambling, *Why* now, What will happen to you - your relationship, your home life, your children, your health - if you don't. Where you'll be in 5 years' time if we don't take action today.

Get LOTS of reasons – the more reasons, the more leverage.

Examples:

I want to stop because I'm sick of losing, sick of being in debt.

I want to stop because if I don't my wife will leave me and I'll be separated from my children. I couldn't stand that.

I want to stop because it's not fun anymore and causes me a lot of stress. I never have any money.

I want to stop because my life will be in shreds if I don't. I'll probably end up in prison or worse.

Be as SPECIFIC as possible, and write down several reasons. When you've done it read it out loud to yourself.

#4 - **Accept** that Gambling is causing Problems in your Life

Read the following statements out loud, and say it like you mean it. Tell your brain what the new rules are.

"I am ready to accept that... "

> *I don't gamble normally, and that it's out of control.*
>
> *Gambling is causing problems in my life and that my life has become unmanageable.*
>
> *I know that I exceed every limit I set myself, every time. I don't want to, but I do.*

[If when reading these statements you feel they are NOT true, then you are still under the illusion that you have some control over your gambling.

You need to **STOP** reading this book here and should not proceed any further. It will not help you - actually it *cannot* help you, until you are ready to admit that you have a problem. If you've done the first 3 exercises in this section and still think you can control your gambling, then go back and get some more.

Or go back to Page 1 and start reading again, this time reading it properly and answering the 20 Questions honestly and doing each of the Exercises.]

* * *

SUMMARY

EXERCISE: Write down your NUMBERS
(Total Time and Total Money) and your WHY

Also do the following:

Close your eyes, and imagine walking into a room where you see all your friends and family sitting down. At the front of the room you see a box, and when you look inside the box you realise that it's you and it's your funeral.

Imagine the kinds of things you want people to be saying about you – how do you want to be remembered? What kind of person do you want them to remember you as?

Take the lid off those emotions - See it, Hear it, *Feel* it.

The goal of this section is to ask you to ACCEPT that you have a problem and know WHY you must take action now.

If don't have these two things then do not read the rest of this book, but instead go back to gambling until you are ready to look at the facts honestly. This might take months or possibly years of more misery, but it is your choice – you're the one that has to pay the price.

Chapter 12
The Benefits of Recovery

Before we get into it, let's just remember WHY we want to do something about our gambling. This is going to take some effort, so we need to get some leverage on ourselves.

Below are things that others have written about what they want in their life, that gambling is stopping them from having. Can you identify with any? Make a note of the ones that would mean the most to you if you were able to get them, to feel them regularly in your life.

1. Clearer thinking

2. More focus

3. Less mood swings

4. Sharper mental dexterity

5. More articulate

6. Better memory

7. Working through stress more effectively

8. Increased energy levels

9. Reduced depression

10. Deeper interactions with others

11. Improved integrity

12. Boosted confidence

13. No social anxiety

14. Better focus on task at hand

15. Enjoying simple pleasures more deeply

16. Increased ability to control negative mental triggers

17. No risk of arrest or legal troubles

18. Increased joy

19. Renewed self-respect

20. More free time

21. Need to sleep less

22. Treat money with respect

23. Confidence to try new things

24. Increased humility

25. Asking others for help

26. Better partnership with partner

27. Better ability to learn and remember new things

28. Can pay for things without fear of payment failing

29. No worries about of being found out by somebody

30. Be a better parent

31. True bonds with friends

32. Better fitness level

33. New doors opening to spiritual world

34. Confidence to take on any task

35. Less panic attacks

36. No more paranoia

37. Increased motivation for self-improvement

38. Feeling of wholeness that is not reliant on external source

39. Not being enslaved by the need for gambling

40. No more feeling guilty

41. Saving time

42. Communicating more

43. Renewed sense to sensations

44. Have much more energy than before

45. Deeper philosophical thinking

46. Way more patience

47. Increased brainpower and mental endurance

48. Regain of focus to finish one job before starting the next one

49. Waking up in the morning feeling rested

50. The return of sense of self

51. Improved ability to relate

52. Regain of job satisfaction

53. Stronger mental control over moods and thought processes

54. Be more intimate with my partner

55. Experiencing natural highs

56. The ability to inspire other people

57. The development of healthy habits

58. A sharper mental game

59. Increased muscle tone

60. Heightened sense of humour

61. More love of life

62. Better response to emotionally charged situations

63. Renewed sense of life, waking up to greet the morning sun and air

64. Easier to get out of bed

65. Develop a mature, competent coping mechanism

66. Feeling in control always

67. A stronger sense of optimism about life

68. Being better at controlling other aspects of life, like cooking, exercising etc

69. Improved quality of work

70. More present for family and friends

71. More agility and awareness

72. Stop acting like a child and grow up

73. Not constantly craving something every time I get bored or stressed

74. Better health, less sickness

75. Reduced anger

76. Better communication of feelings

77. Dramatic improvement of self-esteem

78. Being a more interesting person

79. Clearer memories

80. Share more laughs

81. No more panic attacks

82. Feeling of more freedom

83. Better teamwork

84. Reduced anxiety

85. Be better role model for my kids

86. Sleep better

87. The joy of making things happen and being powerful;

88. Enjoying the daylight and sunlight

89. Enjoying the observation of lives around

90. Better emotional health

91. Emotional energy savings

92. Feel intense emotions without being ruled by them

93. Strength to keep going when the going gets tough

94. Keep my promises

95. Enjoy a relaxed mental state

96. Improved courage

97. Less nightmares

98. Increased trust

99. Joy of sharing

100. Success.

* * *

EXERCISE: Write down at least 10 short goals that YOU want in your life, that Gambling is preventing you from having.

As you write each, VISUALISE how great it would to have that something in your life today, right now.

Chapter 13
Safeguards

The following are tried and tested barriers, things that make it difficult for you to gamble in the early days. Over the years hundreds of thousands, perhaps millions of gamblers have used these safeguards to give them some breathing space while they get their life back on track. They're not always easy or pleasant, but they work.

Why do we need these? Well as we were looking at earlier, urges to gamble are something that we act out on automatically, as they trigger the same old programming and use the same old established circuit.

We Gamble simply because we CAN.
We have the Time and Money to do so.

So we need things in place to interrupt the pattern, to prevent us from acting on the urge, to make sure that if an opportunity presents itself that gambling can't just happen on its own every time we get money. We need to disengage the AutoPilot.

In many ways this is probably the hardest part of tackling your gambling problem. Not just because it is the first practical bit, but because it requires some qualities which we haven't used in a long time:

HONESTY and TRANSPARENCY

Enlist a Helper

Ideally you are going to need the help of someone close to you – a partner, mother, father, aunt, friend, etc. Things might already be strained with this person, but you need to ask their help. Getting them a copy of this book will educate them, answer a lot of their questions, and help get them onside.

If there is no-one that can help you, then try harder! Just because you don't *want* to do something, or don't like it, doesn't means you *can't* do it. You have a full-blown addiction and half measures just won't cut it, sorry.

Only if you are an orphan with no friends or family, should you handle your own money in these early stages. That gambler voice in you that is saying you *don't need safeguards, you understand now, you'll be fine, you can handle it,* etc is the same voice that you have been listening to for a long time – the one that keeps you gambling and tells you that it is going to be different this time (but it never is, is it).

So dial that voice down for the moment and let's get some temporary barriers in place. Doing some of these things are pretty scary, but you'll feel SO much better once you've done them. With each one you are actually *doing* something about your gambling problem and taking back control of your future.

And DO NOT give your Helper a hard time – you need their help, so don't blow it. You might feel like a child, but try not to act like one!

#1 – Money

A Compulsive Gambler needs TIME and MONEY. Without one or the other, it's difficult to place the first bet - and without the first the second one can't happen, or the third. First let's set about tying up the money, just for now.

- ACCESS – A gambler needs money, or access to money, in order to gamble. So the sooner you are cut off from it the better. You know that if you have it you'll only gamble until your last pound is gone, as you always do. Give it to someone else to hold onto for you (partner, mother, father, aunt, friend, etc). It's not even money to us – it's spins/credits/chips, tokens, etc. It will still be *your* money, just looked after by someone else.

- WAGES - Have your wages/benefits/rent paid direct into your Helper's account. No IF'S or BUT's. Around

80% of gamblers fail at this point, thinking that they can still handle their own money. You can in the long term, but for the moment you need zero access.

- BANK – Open an account with a bank that can be set to block gambling transactions. Two good ones are Monzo and Starling Bank. Open either a current account or a joint account with your Helper, and only keep the money that you need to get you through the day in it. Do not put all your wages in, or despite your best intentions it could turn out like it like before. Once your new account with Monzo or Starling is enabled, make sure that gambling blocks are enabled on the account.

- CARDS – Hand over your cards to your Helper – ALL of them. Make sure all the statements are delivered to your home address. The only card you should be carrying is the Monzo/Starling card which contains a small amount of money, and only what you *need* (not want).

- CASH – Only carry the *exact* cash you need for that day, and get receipts for everything you spend and give them back to your appointed Bank Manager. Even better use your Monzo / Starling card for all payments, so your Helper can see all your transactions.

- DEBTS - Every Problem Gambler runs up debts. We all ignore bank statements and phone calls, hiding our heads in the sand. It's all just too stressful. We self-medicate this stress with yet more gambling, making the problem worse - it's a vicious circle. You will need your Helper to contact the debtors with you (see Managing Debts in the Appendix).

- BILLS – Sit down with your Helper and get all your bills and living costs written down or in a spreadsheet. Work out what you're behind on and write to the provider if required. Make proposals to pay arrears over time.

- FOOD & FUEL – Ask your helper to help fill you up with fuel, stock up food, etc on a weekly basis so you know you have basics covered and don't have to handle the money yourself.

No doubt the Gambler inside you is already kicking off, telling you that this is inconvenient, unnecessary or embarrassing. This is normal but you MUST follow through and start protecting your income. It's still yours, but you just won't have direct access to it.

Remember it's not for ever, but IS essential for now.

#2 - Gambling Blocks

You can get software / Apps that stop gambling on devices and PC's. They were literally made for YOU, so go get one and install it today, right now. Yet another barrier in place.

Do a Google search or App Store search for 'gambling blocker' or 'gambling block software' to find current ones. Also search reviews so that you know you are going for one that actually works (some of them are easy to uninstall or get around).

While you're at it delete any gambling Apps on your phone, and pass the phone to your Helper to setup Parental Controls on your phone/tablet with their own secret PIN. Importantly tell them that you should not be able to install Apps from the AppStore on your own phone, or you'll soon be discovering Gambling Apps. The parental controls should be implemented for all devices – not for ever, just for now.

[I will post a list of decent ones on GamblingAddiction.blog]

#3 - Self-Exclusion

Time to ban yourself from where you currently gamble - Websites, Betting Shops, Casinos, Arcades, etc.

DO NOT DO THIS ON YOUR OWN. With betting shops or casinos have someone physically go in with you to get the forms, then go back again to post them through the door. Even better get someone to get a self-exclusion form for you, fill it in at home, then submit by post. For online, have someone sit with you while you do it so they can see you've done it.

With any physical exclusion form always include your own covering letter with scanned photo, stating:

- Your full name, home address, and date of birth
- State that you are an existing customer who has a gambling problem
- State that you wished to be banned permanently from their site / premises / etc and all sites / establishments run by their organisation
- Name, Signature and date

Then go onto GAMSTOP.CO.UK which is the new self-exclusion service. Register and do what it asks. Note that at the time of writing GamStop is *not* a completely effective solution, but it is being improved slowly.

So in addition to GamStop, it's really important to go through the manual steps above listed above. It's hard work, but also helps instruct your subconscious mind that Enough is Enough.

* * *

SUMMARY

It's tempting to think you don't need to do all that, isn't it? I was like that too.

But over the 25 years I probably saw in the region of 1,500 problem gamblers try to free themselves from gambling. Those that put ALL the safeguards in place had a **95% success rate**. Those that didn't bother with them had around a **5% chance**.

And those that only put some of the safeguards in place also failed, as they left easy loopholes open which they would always exploit.

A Gambler needs TIME and MONEY. The Addicts that tied them *both* up gave themselves the best chance at beating this.

Many of the 90% that failed disappeared, and would come back to the groups 3-5 years later having lost a load more money, relationships, jobs, self respect – the usual story. Their gambling had got worse too.

So work out for yourself if you want to keep gambling, or if you really are ready to get off the rollercoaster once and for all.

Chapter 14
Understanding Your Triggers

There are daily Events and Emotions that set us off, that start the gambling circuit running in our brains, known in psychological terms as *Cues*. Another commonly used word for these is *Triggers*.

When we're gambling a lot of different things can trigger our behaviour, some conscious and some unconscious. Once we know what our some of our triggers are, we can work around them so they don't bother us. Untriggered triggers lose their power and attention over time.

A good place to start is by listing two columns, one for *Feelings* and the other for *Events*. On the next page are some examples, but think about it yourself and write as much as you can that is personal to you.

EMOTIONS	TRIGGER EVENT
I often Gamble when I feel:	*Gambling often follows these activities or events:*
Anxious	See gambling Ads on TV
Stressed	See gambling Ads on my Phone
Bored	Being on my Own
Alone	Deadlines
Sorry for Myself	After Kids have gone to bed
	Paying Bills
	Seeing a Bank
	Seeing a Bookies
	Hearing a Machine Payout in a Pub
	Watching football on Sky Sports

Once you have your own list, look down the columns and see how an *Event* might trigger an *Emotion*.

For example, *Seeing a Bank*, or *Paying Bills* always make me feel *Stressed.*

Maybe *Being on my Own* often makes me feel *Lonely* and *Sorry for Myself*.

And perhaps *Hearing a Machine Payout in a Pub* sometimes makes me *Anxious.*

You get the idea. We're not going to do anything about these Triggers just yet, other than know that they exist and perhaps do what we can to avoid them.

Below are some sample ways of avoiding the trigger or minimising our exposure to it. The key thing is to work out NOW how you intend to react, and not at the time that the urge arrives - that'll be too late.

Pen and paper time!

EMOTIONS & TRIGGERS	REPLACEMENT ACTION
Anxious	Talk to someone!
Stressed	Go for a walk / to the gym!
Bored	Do something quick!
Lonely	Go find people / pick up phone, call friend!
Sorry for Myself	Read something that inspires me!
Seeing gambling Ads on TV	Change channel fast / walk out room!
Gambling Ads on my Phone	Turn off phone! Avoid Facebook!
Being on my Own	Call friends and visit!
Football	Avoid for a month or two! Cancel Subscription!
Deadlines	Discuss with boss / team!
After Kids in bed	Plan time to fill the void! New hobby / challenge!
Paying Bills	Don't do it on my own!
Seeing a Bank	Look the other way!
Seeing a Bookies	Walk other side of street!
Hearing a Machine Payout	Don't stand near machine! Choose different pub! Stay away from the pub for the moment!

The above list is mostly the list of things that used to set *me* off, and what I used to do instead. But write your own that is personal to YOU.

The trick with this is to write them as if you are advising a good friend, how to keep THEM safe. And if they're good enough for a friend, they're good enough for you.

Do whatever it takes! If you have to give certain things a wide berth for a while in order to get over your addiction, then so be it. If it helps you get your head straight then friends will understand – everyone just wants you to get better.

See your reluctance to implement sensible alternatives as your inner gambler fighting for control – don't listen and don't give in!

* * *

HOMEWORK

Fill out *your* list of Triggers, both for Emotions and Events.

Then write out a fresh list of Immediate Actions you would like to take when each of those Events or Emotions come up. Create alternatives, several of them.

Mentally rehearse each one in your mind - it will help your brain remember these new actions and call on them when you need them. If it helps carry the list with you.

FIVE

DAILY

ROUTINES

for a

NEW LIFE

Don't be selective - try <u>ALL</u> of them
and you stand the best chance of repairing your life
in the shortest possible time.

They will give you Structure and keep your thinking straight
helping you to be happy and productive

One Day at a Time

Chapter 15
Morning Routine

The happiest and most successful people on the planet have a Morning Routine. They don't just roll out of bed and let the day happen to them - they let the day know who's in charge!

Within 90 minutes of waking up they have already conditioned their brain and sometimes even their body. So if their day goes to **** they have already achieved something.

And if your brain's already starting to make excuses like *"I don't have time"* then get up a few minutes earlier and MAKE time – it's important.

What Should my Morning Routine look like?

1. **Make your Bed** – this is an old army trick that sets up your subconscious to be in control. Why does this work? If you want to get anything big done (like get through the day in a war zone) then split the big task into lots of smaller tasks, and get the first thing off the list as quickly as humanly possible. The first thing on

your morning list is your bed – so do it quickly and make it look good. Note this tactic and use it in other aspects of your recovery, too.

2. **Exercise** – This can be a 10-20 minute walk, a few press ups or situps, or a full-on proper workout. But do *something*. Exercise is extremely good at reconditioning addicted brains, while naturally producing the same kind of endorphins that gambling creates. So get into the habit as it will make you feel good and like you've accomplished something. Have a refreshing shower after.

3. **Gratitude** – Sit quietly for 10-20 minutes and try to get a better perspective on your life. Close your eyes, breath deeply, and place both hands over your heart. Say *"thank you"* to yourself (out loud or in your head) and how grateful you are for your heart, which was given to you freely and beats 100,000 times a day. It enables you to live.

Move your thoughts out to the rest of your body, giving thanks to anything you choose (Universe, God, or yourself) for what you have. Then move your thoughts out further to your family, friends & animals, again *feeling* the love you have for each of them, saying *Thank you* for each of them. Really mean it and feel it.

Finally move out to material things in your life - your home, career, and anything else that you feel deserves a Thank You and that you are grateful for. Sounds crazy but you'll feel good.

4. **Affirmations** – An affirmation is a statement that you make to yourself as if you already possess that something. For instance, a person who is not particularly confident might say *"I am confident"*. Affirmations are amazing as they help communicate with, and reprogram, our subconscious. Crazy I know, but your brain actually accepts them as instructions, but only if there is emotional intensity- so say it with FEELING.

While we are still sitting we are going to breathe deeply and regularly, and make the following affirmations, repeating each one out loud **x5 times** and with *feeling*, then move onto the next. **And say it like you mean it, like your life depends on it.** I don't care how stupid you might feel - this is a prime way to reprogram your subconscious and stimulate new circuit growth.

"EVERYTHING I NEED IS WITHIN ME NOW"

"I AM UNAFRAID, AND AS I GIVE TO WORLD SO THE WORLD GIVES BACK TO ME"

"I AM HONEST, I AM TRUTHFUL, I AM TRANSPARENT, I AM ME."

With each repetition change the focus and emphasis to a different word:

EVERYTHING I NEED IS WITHIN ME **NOW**.
EVERYTHING I NEED IS WITHIN **ME** NOW.
EVERYTHING I NEED IS WITHIN ME NOW.
EVERYTHING I **NEED** IS WITHIN ME NOW.

Say it with a rhythm as if you are skipping.

[You can also do this throughout the day, in the car for example - with your eyes open, obviously! Affirmations said repeatedly with feeling reprogram your subconscious – that part of your brain that is telling you to run away to the safety and comfort of gambling. THEY WORK – try them for a week or two and see the change.]

5. **Breakfast** – Eat a healthy, balanced breakfast and feel good about your mind and your body. Set your brain up for repair. Pay special attention to some of the Dopamine and Serotonin rich foods in the Exercise & Diet section, and top up your neurotransmitters before the day even starts.

* * *

How Does Having a Morning Routine Help?

When we're gambling, everything is somewhere between unstructured freeform - going with the flow, trusting in the inspiration of the moment - and chaos. Your new morning routine helps you start your day with structure (which your addicted brain needs) and puts in motion some key elements to carry through the next 12 hours.

- **Making your bed** gets you your first natural Dopamine reward of the day, as your first achievement of the day is under your belt

- **Exercise** helps generate Dopamine, Serotonin and Endorphins, and reduces Cortisol – so you feel great with less stress

- **Gratitude** generates high levels of Serotonin, helping you feel calm and content. It also helps embed a new brain pattern – one where the glass isn't half empty, but half full. This will help affect all other thinking and begins a virtuous circle

- **Breakfast** not only gives you energy and fuels your brain, it reduces the risk of you having low blood sugar which creates body stress and can end up as a craving to gamble. Also when your body and brain are deprived of energy you have high *Cortisol* levels, which prevents your Prefrontal Cortex from working properly (bad judgement, bad decisions etc) and makes it difficult for new Neurons to be generated, along with other negative effects. A good breakfast should also top you

173

up with neurotransmitters reducing urges and thoughts of gambling.

You'll also be getting out your Daily Programme that you wrote last night (more on that shortly) which you could read over breakfast.

Chapter 16
"Just For Today" Programme

The **Just for Today** programme is utilised in many modern-day recovery programmes. Originally written by Frank Crane in 1921 and published in his column in the Boston Globe, it was adopted first by Alcoholics Anonymous and then others including Gamblers Anonymous.

The programme is deceptively simple, yet has so much to teach. It personally helped me get through the good days and the bad, and without a doubt helped recondition and retrain my abnormal mind.

My approach has been to try one of these per day. I say *try* as I am not usually successful in doing it right – and therein lies the lesson it has to teach me and that I have yet to learn. Much of my own learning & recovery over the 25 years is thanks to this simple programme – try it.

Prescription: ONE a day without fail (*thank you Dr. Crane*) in any order you like. Rotate daily. This needs to be one of your *"new"* habits. A simple yet effective way of retraining your brain and installing new behaviours.

Just for today I will have a Daily Program. I may not follow it exactly, but I will have it. I will save myself from two pests: hurry and indecision.

Just for today I will try to live through this day only, and not tackle all my problems at once. I can do something for twelve hours that would appal me if I felt I had to keep it up for a lifetime.

Just for today I will be happy. Happiness is a state of mind and most people are as happy as they make up their minds to be.

Just for today I will adjust myself to what is, and not try to adjust everything to my own desires. I will take my "luck" as it comes, and fit myself to it.

Just for today I will try to strengthen my mind. I will study. I will learn something useful. I will not be lazy. I will read something that requires effort, thought and concentration.

Just for today I will exercise my soul in three ways: I will do somebody a good turn, and not get found out (if anyone knows of it, it won't count). I will do at least two things I don't want to do – just for exercise. I will not show anyone that my feelings are hurt - they may be hurt, but today I will not show it.

Just for today I will be agreeable. I will look as well as I can, dress becomingly, keep my voice low, be courteous, and not be critical. I won't find fault with anything, nor try to improve or regulate anybody but myself.

Just for today I will have a quiet half hour all by myself and relax. During this half hour, sometime, I will try to get a better perspective of my life.

Just for today I will not lie. I will be honest, transparent and straightforward, even if it is not as easy as telling people what they want to hear.

Just for today I will be unafraid. Especially I will not be afraid to notice what is beautiful and to believe that as I give to the world, so the world will give to me.

* * *

How Does Doing the Just For Today Help?

When we're gambling, we may want to do things differently but it always ends up the same. Just *attempting* each one of the JFT exercises helps our brain develop in a new way, and by doing so <u>not</u> use the old destructive patterns (which wither and die).

I personally didn't realise how much I had to learn or change until I tried some of these. But they taught me well and change soon followed.

The Just for Today programme is a deceptively simple programme that will help recondition your mind. You'll have happier days and feel less urges too.

Chapter 17
Grown Up Checklist

Wherever there is Gambling Addiction, there are immature, selfish immature behaviour patterns and maybe an underdeveloped brain as well. You may not be a child anymore, but like it or not you are certainly acting like one a lot of the time. I certainly was.

So here's a checklist of things we should be working towards on a daily basis. Acting and reacting in these new ways will help install new "grown up" behaviours, overwrite our old ones, and help our brain fully mature.

Read this checklist list on a daily basis (ideally in the morning) and then be guided by its rules throughout the day. It will help divert our normal behaviour into more productive ones with better outcomes.

1. Adjust myself to other people and their needs – I am not the centre of the universe.

2. Accept criticism gratefully, being honestly glad for an opportunity to improve myself.

3. Do not indulge in feeling sorry for myself, it's a waste of effort.

4. Don't expect special consideration from anyone, I am no more important than anyone else.

5. Control my temper, as it will get me into trouble.

6. Stay calm and meet emergencies with poise.

7. Don't allow my feelings to be easily hurt - I am an adult now, time to act like one.

8. Accept responsibility for my own actions.

9. Time to outgrow the all or nothing stage.

10. Recognise that no person or situation is wholly good or bad, and that there is usually a middle ground.

11. Be patient at reasonable delays, without stamping my feet.

12. Endure defeat and disappointment without whining or complaining.

13. Not worry about things I cannot help.

14. Not show off or boast in annoying or unwelcome ways.

15. Be honestly glad when others enjoy success or good fortune. It's time to outgrow envy and jealousy.

16. Listen thoughtfully to the opinions of others, to be open minded, and not become argumentative when my views are opposed.

17. Not be a chronic fault finder, but take a more balanced view.

18. Plan things in advance, rather than trusting to the inspiration of the moment.

19. Not view my whole life problem at once, instead focus on today and what I can control.

20. Not blame others for my past, present or future.

Accept that the past is gone – we cannot get it back.

Accept that the money has gone too, and draw a line under it.

The future hasn't been written yet
and can be whatever we choose to make it.

Make the best of today, and feel grateful for what we have.

---

* * *

How does Acting like a Grown Up Help?

Nobody likes to think of themselves as acting childishly (not even children!)

But it's become such a habit that we don't realise how childish our gambling addiction must make us behave. And the consequences of those childish actions. Or is it the other way around - that our immature childlike approach results in gambling? We avoid problems with gambling. Either way it needs work. Disappointments and frustrations create urges to gamble. Gambling is a little "ME" time which turns into a LOT of "ME" time. These are not the actions of a mature person – or if they were the world would be a real mess!

So read this checklist every morning and keep an eye on your behaviour, changing it to a more mature one as we react to the events of the day.

One thing is certain - if we do a good enough impression of a grown up on a daily basis, our brains automatically create the neural patterns needed to support the new behaviour. We might just make it to adulthood one day, regardless of our real age.

But remember that to become a proper adult we still need to build out a multi-centred way of life with some more equal attention on Work, Family, Partner, Recreation and Exercise so that our life has multiple areas that nurture us and others in different ways.

Chapter 18
The Six Human Needs
(as a daily programme)

To recap, everyone has Six Human Needs:

Certainty   Feeling Secure

Uncertainty / Variety Feeling challenged

Significance   Feeling recognised / important

Love / Connection   Feeling connected and nurtured

Growth   Constantly developing

Contribution   Giving to others

Check back in <u>Chapter 10</u> for the full description and details.

Working the Six Human Needs on a daily basis
is done in two ways, each as important as the other.

#1 - Working the Programme FOR YOURSELF

Your mission (should you choose to accept it) is to make a list of the first <u>FOUR</u> needs, and:

- Write out how you meet them. Think about what gambling does for you, and perhaps which need(s) you are using Gambling as a substitute for the real thing.

- Write down how you would LIKE to meet these needs in an ideal world. In what happier, healthier ways *could* you meet them, that would help you become the person that you want to become.

#2 - Working the Programme FOR SOMEONE ELSE

Repeat the above, but this time it's not about you, it's all about *them* - your Partner, your Children, whoever you choose. If we want to get over an immature and selfish addiction like gambling, then we <u>have </u>to stop focussing inward on ourselves and start facing outward on others and *their* needs. This will help *our* brains repair and our behaviours improve.

- For each important person in your life, write down how you currently help meet THEIR needs. Think about how gambling prevents you from doing more.

- Write down how you would LIKE to meet each of their needs if you could, and how that might help them:

How can you help them feel more *secure*? What could you do to add a little more *variety* into their day?

- How would you like to make them feel a little more noticed, more *appreciated*? Do they feel enough *love* from you? How could you show them more?

Meeting Other People's Needs

If you satisfy:

TWO of someone's needs, you have a *connection*.

FOUR of someone's needs, you have a *strong attachment*.

SIX of someone's needs, the person is *permanently bonded to you*.

Gambling is an entirely *selfish activity* where we are constantly consumed with ourselves. We know this because of the amount of lies we have to tell to keep it a secret.

A good starting point to recovering our own personality is to start meeting the needs of the others, however we can. Don't overdo it as they might have been badly treated by you, and treat a lot of what you say and do with a fair amount of caution! That's to be expected.

A good place to start is just letting them know that you are making an effort, by asking them if they need help with anything. Or just help without asking them.

* * *

How Does Working the Six Human Needs Help?

When we're gambling, we've got a one-track mind focussed on ME, ME, ME. And we don't even do a good job of that! We gamble so much that it shapes our personality into something that is distorted, out of balance. We feel empty and shallow, hollow and unfulfilled and think that another win will somehow fill that gap.

The Six Human Needs is a simple framework for rebalancing ourselves, enabling us to see consider how we are meeting our needs in healthy or unhealthy ways. It reminds us that **balance** is the natural state of all things, and challenges us to do better in certain areas.

When we apply Human Needs thinking to others, it not only helps them but helps *us* become more centred and fulfilled as a person.

And if we do a good enough *impression* of a grown up, our brain will automatically create the underlying neural patterns needed to support the new behaviour, and gradually we become one.

Chapter 19
Daily Programme

From now on you are going to have a "Daily Programme": a plan that contains your hour-by-hour intentions for what will happen that day. You will write the Programme the night before and carry it around with you the next day. You may not follow it exactly, but you will have it. Tick things off as you go, which feels satisfying because marking things off a ToDo list automatically generates Dopamine. Our brain rewards good behaviour with a pat on the back!

Trust me, it will help - massively. Instead of seeing how the day turns out and going with the flow (which at some stage might include gambling) you are going to plan your time in advance, hour by hour. You're going to design the kind of day that would give you immense satisfaction if you were able to live it.

What Should I Include in My Programme?

You use this program to plan your day hour by hour, but the great thing is you can incorporate the best bits of the other programmes too. This is your MASTER program.

*Important: You write out your Programme **the night before**.*

*This is your new STRUCTURE
the opposite of the chaos you have been living.*

- **MORNING ROUTINE**: see Morning section

- **TIME:** Hour by hour diary – my morning, work, lunch, work, after work, evening *(avoiding Triggers)* [see Chapter 14]

- **MONEY:** Plan how much I will need for transport, food etc [see Chapter 13]

- **JUST FOR TODAY** – Pick the next one on the list and try to do it throughout the day [see Chapter 16]

- **SIX HUMAN NEEDS** – As well as my own, can I help meet someone else's needs today? [see Chapter 18]

- **MINDFULNESS** – Schedule in 20 minutes of quiet reflection but also do the odd bit here and there [see Chapter 21]

- **EXERCISE** – Include at least 20 minutes of exercise like a walk, gym, bike, swim, class, etc [see Chapter 24]

- **DIET** - Pay attention to Diet throughout the day in order to keep your neurotransmitters topped up naturally, and keep yourself properly hydrated too [see Chapter 24]

> *Write out your Daily Programme*
> *the **night before** without fail - told you twice!*

Your goal is to actually *follow through* on what you want to do today, not have it hijacked by gambling. To have lived a **Multi-Centred** day and feel like you've achieved something, for one day only. This is the complete polar opposite of spending several hours you don't have on gambling (with money you don't have) then having to cover it up afterwards, and being stressed out.

And if, despite our best planning and intentions, it all goes to **** then we'll just learn from it and start again tomorrow.

Don't beat yourself up - **Breath in, Breath out, Plough on.** It gets easier.

Plan Time with Others

Gamblers usually gamble alone, and often choose to work for themselves or on their own in order that they can feed their gambling habit.

So when writing out your plan, make sure it involves others. The more time you spend in the company of others, the less at risk of gambling you will be. It's a great physical way to break your pattern and re-socialise yourself at the same time.

Don't Forget your Six Human Needs!

Give extra thought to which of your Six Needs you might have already identified as needing work. Balance is the key. For instance, you might want to schedule time with your partner or children.

When writing out your daily programme, think about *their* needs also and how you could help meet them.

* * *

How Does Having a Daily Programme Help?

When we're gambling, we have no *structure*. Instead we have the opposite - *chaos*. And before we know it, gambling just happened again – resulting in yet more chaos. In fact we're on a white-knuckle ride on the rollercoaster of chaos.

So our immature, underdeveloped, scattered brain needs a more organised, structured approach that gets us off that rollercoaster and restore some sanity. One that brings together many of the techniques and approaches in this book, which if used on a daily basis will result in *massive* changes to our minds and circumstances.

Our daily programme:

- Keeps us on track and focussed
- Avoids triggers which hijack our day (and have a list of alternative Actions)
- Helps generate feel-good Dopamine when we cross another ToDo off our list
- Helps us meet new challenges, growing new brain cells and establishing new healthy patterns
- Keeps us away from gambling and the old destructive habits

Personally, I couldn't have got over my gambling problem without it.

For the first 3 years off gambling, having a **Daily Programme** kept me focussed and on track, and prevented me slipping back into my old ways.

And while others were having urges, slipping up and going back to gambling, I wasn't. Instead I was actually *living* for once. On my bad days (of which there were many) having a daily programme steered me through. Even just *having* one made me feel better.

When I look back over the years, the times when I worked a daily programme were the happiest, most productive days of my life. Days in which I learned about who I could become without the gambling. And it gave me the courage and perspective to actually *do it*.

In contrast, the days where I thought I was too busy to write my programme or that I didn't need one were the most unproductive days, even though I wasn't gambling!

So I highly recommend it - it worked for me. Having a Programme helped me rewire my dysfunctional brain one day at a time, and rebuild my life - a day at a time.

FIVE WAYS

to

REPAIR AND UPGRADE YOUR MIND

MINDFULNESS

MANAGING STATE

NEURO-ASSOCIATIVE CONDITIONING

DIET & EXERCISE

JOINING A TRIBE

Chapter 20

A Brief Introduction to (Re)programming Your Addicted Brain

When a person's brain is in a state of addiction, they will behave like an addict and suffer all the negative consequences of addiction.

But when a person's brain is NOT in a state of addiction, they will NOT behave like an addict and therefore NOT suffer all the negative consequences of addiction, right?

The good news is that the brain has high plasticity and is capable of rewiring itself from one state to the other. Most people believe this reprogramming can take place in 30-90 days, when a new habit can be installed and the old one overwritten.

So the "cure" (if there is such is thing) is actually getting your brain to reprogram itself, installing new behaviours over old patterns. I used to joke that I needed a brain transplant. Well, this is the next best thing.

In this section I am going to take you through five proven ways of achieving this. They all work. You can and should do all five, but at the very least choose THREE and put everything you can into doing them.

If you're ready to sort this out once & for all, then read on. But if you're not quite there yet then stop here, and come back when you've had enough of gambling and ARE prepared to do whatever it takes. Reading the methods won't make any difference - having a go at DOING them will.

Will these Techniques Work?

I only personally recommend things that proven to 100% work, and that deliver real results. But to make them work you need to **raise your standards** – it's time to turn your *Shoulds* into *MUSTS*.

How Long Will It Take?

That's totally up to you and how much effort you put in. Your brain will change most rapidly if you follow the exercises and really <u>FEEL</u> the pain of not changing. Repeat the exercises over and over and feel the change. FEEL the pain that you are moving away from, and FEEL the benefits of what you're moving towards – it's the *emotion* that causes your brain's neurons and synapses to remap and rewire themselves rapidly.

Actually *Feeling* our emotions – not avoiding them – is what makes the change happen rapidly, as this stimulates the brain to create new neural pathways that ensure our future survival. Right now your subconscious thinks that Gambling is essential to your survival - we're going to help it believe otherwise. Anything we feel intensely is given top priority by our mind. So turn up the intensity, give yourself permission to change, and welcome it.

But if you just read it without feeling and think "*Okay, yes, I suppose I should probably change..*" then it will take x50 times longer and your problems are not behind you yet.

No **feeling** = No **intensity** = No **result**.

So if you want to rid yourself of your Gambling Addiction once and for all, and be able to think and feel normally again, then get ready to find out how.

Deep breath - you have nothing to fear, and absolutely *everything* to gain.

I've got a 25-year headstart on you and can tell you that it's absolutely worth it. At first, getting through the day without gambling was like learning to walk again. But even after the first week I was feeling the fog lift and some sense that I was on the mend.

* * *

Chapter 21
Mindfulness

*Mindfulness is paying attention in a particular way:
on purpose, in the present moment, without judgement.*

Kabat-Zinn, 1994

The mind of a gambler is always racing from problem to problem, from bet to bet, debt to debt. In fact it hardly ever stops and we feel worn out a lot of the time. This constantly stressed state becomes normal, and even sleep evades us.

If someone lives like this for months, years, maybe even decades, there is damage to that person's brain. MRI scans show that some parts are completely overworked and at breaking point, whereas other parts of the brain are hardly utilised. Let's not even get into blood pressure and heart problems!

But there is an easy way to repair the damage, to rebalance the mind and the body.

Mindfulness is a powerful way to put the brakes on your spinning, panicked mind and to observe and interrupt your triggers as they happen.

What is Mindfulness?

"Mindfulness is the basic human ability to be fully present, aware of where we are and what we're doing, and not be overly reactive or overwhelmed by what's going on around us.

While mindfulness is something that we all naturally possess, it's more readily available to us when we practice on a daily basis.

Whenever you bring awareness to what you're directly experiencing via your senses, or to your state of mind via your thoughts and emotions, you're being mindful. And there's growing research showing that when you train your brain to be mindful, you're actually remodelling the physical structure of your brain."

Taken from the excellent Mindful.org

Mindfulness is used to treat a number of psychological problems like stress, depression, anxiety, nervousness, fear, phobias, addiction, compulsive disorders and so on. It helps us disengage from automatic thoughts, habits, and unhealthy behaviour patterns.

De-Stressing & Re-Wiring

By doing even a few seconds of Mindfulness, your stress levels will have just reduced (more if you had done it longer, obviously) and your brain's *"fight or flight"* centre, the *Amygdala*, will have shrunk a little. This primal region of the brain, associated with fear and emotion, is involved in the initiation of the body's response to stress.

As the Amygdala shrinks, the pre-frontal cortex becomes thicker (improving things like awareness, concentration and decision-making).

The *functional connectivity* between these regions – how often they are activated together – also changes. The connection between the Amygdala and the rest of the brain gets weaker, while the connections between areas associated with attention and concentration get stronger.

So Mindfulness, simple as it seems, has the magic to reset everything back to optimal if performed regularly.

But as you will hear me say often, you don't get fit by going to gym once! So if you want to feel the benefits of Mindfulness and have the brain to go with it, then practice it regularly several times a day, and see if you can build up to 10-15 minutes in total.

Pattern Interrupt

Consider what happens when we get a gambling urge. Actually, it's less like a habit and more like a *reflex* – we get the urge, we act out on it. Rinse and repeat hundreds or thousands of times.

But if gambling is a stress response, a need for self-medication, a desire to not be present in our own self, an escape… then Mindfulness is the opposite: *not* running but staying still, being present in the moment and calmly observing thoughts and emotions as they bubble up and float away.

As you have proved over many months and years, being afraid of these thoughts and emotions as they come up, ignoring them, and pushing them back down does *not* get rid of them. They just come back - in fact they come back stronger. You know this as your need for escape gets stronger, and it takes more and more gambling to numb it up too.

On the other hand, *pausing* for a second and observing the urge, understanding *what triggered it* to appear at this precise time, are the keys to releasing it so it no longer bothers you.

By *listening* to your urges and cravings you will quickly understand which specific areas of your life need attention. And small actions in these areas will yield massive results.

GAMBLING	MINDFULNESS
A Stress Response	Switching Focus to the Mind and Body
A Desire to not be present in your own self	Being Present in the Moment
An Escape	Being still, letting your Body catch up with Mind
Numbing up Feelings/Emotions	Calmly Observing Thoughts, Breathe through it
A Method of Self-medication	Asking What, Why
Act Out on Urge	Decide on a Different Course of Action
RESULT	**RESULT**
More Debt, More Stress, More Lies..	*Problems still there, but did not make worse!*
Same old tired cycle, same result..	*Break the cycle, fresh learning about why I gamble!*
More Chaos..	*Temporary Peace!*

Mindfulness Meditation

To start with just try this for 2 minutes only. Then add a minute a day until you've made it to 15 minutes. Don't expect to get it right first time, daily repetition is the key.

1. **Set aside some time** (ideally in the morning). You don't need a meditation cushion or bench, or any sort of special equipment to access your mindfulness skills - but you do need to set aside some time and space. Sit upright, comfortably, breathing deeply and regularly. Imagine breathing IN oxygen, peace and light through the nose, and breathing OUT stress, worry and negative thoughts through the mouth.

2. **Observe the present moment as it is.** The aim of mindfulness is *not* quieting the mind, or attempting to achieve a state of eternal calm. The goal is simple: aim to pay attention to the present moment, without judgment.

3. **Scan your body slowly** from your toes to the top of your head, focussing your attention on your calves, thighs, stomach, chest, arms, neck and head. As you come to a new part focus your attention on it, tense or stretch it, and release. Mentally check how it feels and move onto the next part.

4. **Let your judgments roll by.** When we notice judgments arise during our practice, just make a mental note of them, and let them pass.

5. **Return to observing the present moment** as it is, and our breathing. Our minds often get carried away in thought. That's why mindfulness is the practice of returning, again and again, to the present moment.

6. **Be kind to your wandering mind.** Don't judge yourself for whatever thoughts crop up, just practice recognising when your mind has wandered off, and gently bring it back.

Fight or Flight

There's no let-up on the never-ending rollercoaster of Gambling Addiction. Every hour can be stressful. Bills and letters that we want to hide from and calls that we want to avoid are a daily event. Arguments, disappointments, and discussions about money all do the same. Our Triggers will do it every time.

What you feel in these moments is known as your *Fight or Flight* response - an ancient evolutionary stress response which ensured caveman's survival when being chased or attacked.

The heart beats faster, pupils dilate, and the skin becomes pale or flushed. We are starting to panic, and our nervous system stimulates the Adrenal glands to release Catecholamines (which contain *Noradrenaline*).

Catecholamines also inform our old friend the Amygdala (Fear and Memory centre) which gets freaked out. Due to the surge of adrenaline, the body is now ready to react to the danger, by either fighting it or running from it.

For a Problem Gambler these things create immediate stress, to which our response is nearly always to:

- Self-medicate (using gambling)
- Run away (to gambling)
- Distract and avoid (with gambling)

This might escalate into a full-blown Panic Attack where your heart is beating rapidly that you break out in a cold sweat. But it's just the stress trying to get your attention.

"Pain is a warning that something's wrong"

Madonna, Power of Goodbye

Once you acknowledge it for what it is, it can take 20 to 60 minutes to return to pre-arousal levels.

About 8 years into my 10 year gambling stretch, I experienced panic attacks. I literally felt like I was going to die, like I would have a heart attack any minute and that would be it, game over. I couldn't walk into a room with new people it, and was worried that my mind and now my body were no longer working right.

But when I didn't run and asked myself *"What's the worst that can happen?"* the feeling would start to subside. And using basic Mindfulness to bring my focus back to my breathing helped to.

Mindfulness on the Go

Practicing Mindfulness at moments throughout your day both stimulates the brain's Prefrontal Cortex and reduces activity in your Amygdala, which is central to switching on your stress response. So Mindfulness *immediately* reduces your stress levels, and wakes up the 'Sleeping Policeman' to activate your decision making ability. *Suddenly you are capable of saying NO, whereas before you were not.*

Noticing the stress or the urge as early as possible makes it easier to handle. As soon as you feel an urge to gamble or feel like running away:

1. **Take a deep breath and get curious about what you're feeling.** Scan your body to work out whereabouts in your body you are feeling the urge or the stress.

2. **Write down some details about the urge** on a piece of paper, in a journal, or in a phone (but only if you not an online gambler).

> WHAT were you doing at the time that triggered it?
> WHERE were you?
> WHEN did it happen?
> WHO were you with?

3. **Imagine you are looking at yourself, and ask what you would rather do if you had a choice?** Write it down, eg.

> Go out for a walk / do some exercise..
> Talk to someone..
> Do a 'Just for Today'..
> Read your Therapy, remind yourself of price paid..

4. **Write down <u>WHY</u> you might choose the new choice,** as opposed to gambling.

5. **Make the Choice -** either go gambling or do the other option *immediately.*

6. **Repeat each of the following Affirmations out loud or in your head x5 times.**

"EVERYTHING I NEED IS WITHIN ME NOW."

"JUST FOR TODAY I WILL BE UNAFRAID."

With each repetition emphasise a different <u>word</u>, for instance:

EVERYTHING I NEED IS WITHIN <u>*ME*</u> NOW,
EVERYTHING I NEED IS WITHIN ME <u>*NOW*</u>,
EVERYTHING I <u>*NEED*</u> IS WITHIN ME NOW etc

Break a Mental Pattern… by Doing Nothing!

[In the NAC section after this there is a more detailed method of reprogramming your mind, but below is the most basic form and an explanation of why it works. A lot of people try this as it is the easiest method of all. Think of this as basecamp before we get to the NAC.]

- You can stop the vicious cycle in an instant, simply by *doing nothing.*
- That teaches your subconscious mind that you're not actually dying without the old habit.
- Your brain learns that threatened feelings might be unpleasant for a second, but do not kill you.

The moment you do nothing a *virtuous* circle begins, and your brain copes with the threatened feeling instead of running away to the usual something.

Building a Virtuous Circle

The first step to healthier habits is to <u>*do nothing*</u> when your Cortisol starts giving you that threatened feeling. Doing nothing goes against your body's deepest impulses, but it empowers you to make changes in your life.

When you do nothing, you have time to generate an alternative.

At first, no alternative looks as good as gambling, obviously. But each time you divert your brain electricity in a new direction, you strengthen your new circuit and the old gambling one becomes weaker. It all starts when you ACCEPT a bad feeling for a moment, instead of rushing to make it go away.

Wouldn't it be great to have an alternative that makes you feel good instantly, but in a healthy way? See Chapter 24 Diet and Exercise for some ideas. When you start to understand how your brain works, you can build more healthier habits with fewer side-effects.

* * *

Chapter 22
Managing Your State

Cravings and withdrawal symptoms are the main reason why people often give up giving up. But it is possible to dismiss them instantly using the following technique.

Introducing the TRIAD

Addict or not, there are 3 things that govern the way we all feel at any given moment:

- Our Body
- Our Focus
- Our Language

Changing even *one* of these can make a difference, but changing ALL THREE can get rid of a craving or an urge within a couple of seconds.

Let's take them in turn and see how we can instantly flick the craving switch to OFF. Hiding under the duvet waiting for the urge to pass is no longer necessary.

#1 - Change Your BODY

Changing the way we are using our physical body is one of the quickest and most effective ways to change our emotional state. The change can be a simple as standing tall, shoulders back, chin slightly down, eyes looking forward & slightly up, or deepening our breath. It could also be doing some star jumps, knocking out some press-ups, going for a walk or run, or doing a downward facing dog.

Our body and emotions are tied, so whenever we move our body, we move the emotions in our body. The word "emotion" is derived from the Latin "emotere" which literally means "energy in motion".

#2 - Change Your FOCUS

If we change what we are focusing on, we change our emotions. If we focus on what is wrong, we have a very different emotional experience from focussing on what is right or good, or could be good. If we focus on what we don't want, again we have a very different emotional experience than if we focus on what we DO want. Change what you focus your attention on, and your emotions will follow the new focus.

If you want to change your focus quickly & effectively, ask yourself any of these 5 questions. Ask them until the urge leaves you.

TIP: The most important aspect of this is to FEEL and EXPERIENCE the emotions intensely as you come up with the answers. Feeling the emotion helps change the state and *anchor* it in, which makes it easier to call up on demand. Emotions accelerate neuron connections and can bring about brain change a lot faster than traditional methods like repetition.

The five questions which can bring about immediate change of focus are:

1. **What are you most HAPPY about in your life right now?** What about that makes you happy? How does that make you feel? Feel the feelings. What else are you feeling happy about? (Repeat)

2. **What are you EXCITED about in your life right now?** What, why? How does that make you feel? FEEL the answers in your mind & body.

3. **What do you feel really GRATEFUL for in your life right now?** Answer the question honestly. How does that make you feel? Come up with a second thing you feel really grateful for. FEEL the feeling.

4. **What are you really PROUD of in your life right now?** What about those things makes you feel proud? How does that make you FEEL? Name another thing in your life that you are most proud of. Feel the feelings.

5. **Who do you LOVE most in your life?** Who loves you? How does that make you FEEL? Step into those emotions

and experience them. Feel the love for that person SO much.

Even though you may not have an urge this second, try these questions and *feel* your state change.

***Feel* it in your Heart.** Feel your Emotions respond - let them talk to you and listen for once. They're telling you that it's time to do things differently.

And as you FEEL those good emotions, clench your left fist really tightly. This *anchors* the feel-good emotions to a physical action of your choosing. Do this exercise (feeling then making a fist) x10 or so times over the course of a week, and the following week you should be able to just squeeze your left fist and immediately feel the good emotions. You will have "*anchored*" it in, linked the feeling to a physical trigger.

The more you do this, the more you anchor the feeling to your mind <u>and</u> body. You will have given yourself your first positive trigger which you can summon at will, a superpower which can destroy any threat.

#3 - Change Your LANGUAGE

We again have the power to change our emotional state when we change the *words* we are using, and the *way* that we are using them.

For instance if I say *"I am drowning in debt"* it has a very different emotional impact than if I say *"I owe money"*.

And if I say *"My life is down the drain"* it gets a very different emotional response from my own brain than *"I've got some challenges ahead"*.

You have a choice when it comes to the language you use, and therefore the type of emotions you feel.

Try it - it works. Next time you feel stressed or have an urge, use the **TRIAD** to change your **Body**, your **Focus** and your **Language**.

* * *

How Does Changing your State Work?

Your neural patterns only fire if they are used. So every time you get the urge to gamble and act on it, you reinforce the pattern and make it stronger.

But changing your state through the TRIAD will mean that the existing neural pattern will no longer get used, no matter how well established. And unused patterns shrink and die.

But if you are going to do it this way, you still need to build out the various aspects of your life. You will have a large "gambling shaped gap" which must be filled with all the old things you have been neglecting, and some new things too. So use the TRIAD in conjunction with the other techniques.

And remembers that your goal shouldn't be to *not* do something, but to DO and CREATE something.

Moving away from the Pain of Addiction towards a Happy, Productive, Fulfilling Life.

Chapter 23

Neuro-Associative Conditioning (NAC)

Wouldn't it be great if we could rewire our own brains, just like reprogramming a computer? Uninstall bad programs that were crashing our device and preventing us from getting things done, and install better ones instead?

A SuperComputer on Your Shoulders

Our amazing brains are capable of processing 30 Billion bits of information a second and consist of around **6,000 miles of wiring**. As we learned earlier, this "wiring" is made up of around **28 Billion neurons** (nerve cells designed to conduct impulses). Each one of these neurons can handle around *1 Million bits* of information, and each neuron connects to others to make up small neural networks, which in turn combine together to carry out larger operations.

This is the same principle as software, where individual lines of code form independent modules to perform specific functions. In a facial recognition system for instance, we might have separate modules for drawing, facial mapping, and storing/retrieving data etc. These modules then all talk to each other to create an artificially intelligent system that can look at a face through a webcam and trawl its database for matches.

The only difference is that a human brain can recognise a face in under one second – substantially faster than the most powerful computer in the world. The brain can only do this because its billions of neurons can attack a problem *simultaneously*. Literally the most powerful processing unit on the planet.

Triggers

If we want to change a particular behaviour, we must look at these modules (physical connections) embedded in our Nervous System, known as *Neuro-Associations*.

As our brains are firing off associations simultaneously, our mind can instantaneously hop from one thing to another. But sometimes these associations can get wired up wrong.

For instance, you are addicted to gambling because your subconscious thinks that it is essential to your survival! It connected magnificent feelings of pleasure and reward with feelings of success and self-worth, and tries to get you more of it all the time. But it ignores the constant failure and frustration, and the negative consequences.

So we'll need to reprogram it.

Neurons that Fire together, Wire together

The brain is a constantly evolving intelligence, creating connections between neurons to help its host organism (us) survive.

Our brains learn. If you stick your hand in the fire, it hurts. Your brain senses the pain and believes it could damage or even kill you. So to help you, your brain's survival module links up the image of fire and the sensation of pain, and associates the word 'Fire' as well.

From that point on every time some shouts 'Fire' or you see 'Fire' or read the word 'Fire', some part of your brain will be activated in this mini-circuit about fire. You will naturally flinch or shudder (or panic if for instance you were once trapped in a house fire).

Take for example a toddler crawling along the top of a red couch. She falls off and learns an important lesson about gravity. But being upset and looking up at the red crouch, her brain considers what happened immediately before the pain, and she quickly works out that red couches are dangerous! Clever girl.

It's only when she falls off a few other things does her brain get further opportunities to evaluate what the *real* cause of the pain was, and update her neural pathways accordingly.

Whenever you experience significant amounts of either **Pain** or **Pleasure**, your brain immediately searches for the cause using the following criteria:

1. **Your brain looks for what was UNIQUE.** What was the likely cause? What was unusual? If you are having unusual feelings, it's logical that there must be an unusual cause.

2. **Your brain looks for something that was happening SIMULTANEOUSLY.** Doesn't it make sense that whatever was happening just before the pleasurable or painful sensation was the cause?

3. **Your brain looks for CONSISTENCY.** Aware of what was unique and what was happening, the brain checks if it has happened before, and if it has re-enforces the pathway.

Neuro-Associations in Gambling

Most Gamblers start with a Win. As I mentioned earlier, I was at Uni in the mid 80's and walked past a machine. Two of my friends were frantic about the fact that *"it was going to drop!!"* and literally begged me for change. I gave them what they needed and then this thing lit up like a fairground, vibrating and chugging out money like it was having some kind of digital orgasm! The whole student union stopped what it was doing, and people asked what had happened and who got *"it"*.

We spent the rest of the day in the bar and all had free drinks – the perfect lazy student afternoon.

Little did I know that, right there and then, my brain had also lit up with a massive rush of Dopamine and that my neuro-associations had been imprinted / programmed with a new shiny set of beliefs, that:

I was lucky.

* *Gambling Machines were good to me.*

* *Gambling was fun and easy.*

* *Gambling made me popular.*

I could get money for nothing.

I could make my friends happy.

Then, without realising it, my subconscious spent the following 10 years trying to recreate that Euphoria, that Identity, that *Big Win Feeling* based on the false premise that gambling gave me everything I wanted, and made me everything that I wanted to be! It considered it to be critical to my survival. My clever brain referenced all those magnificently significant feelings and looked for what happened just before, and came up (correctly) with Gambling.

Even when I wasn't winning (most of the time) my brain was niggling away muttering: *"Never mind, it could be you, you've done it before, you can do it again..."* in search of that magic moment.

It wasn't until I had lost everything, lost everyone, and ended up in court at the age of 28 listening to my Mother make excuses for me in the dock, that my old beliefs were stripped from me. Instead new beliefs were installed, that:

I had crossed a line.

I wasn't able to gamble normally any more.

Gambling was costing me more than I could afford or was prepared to pay.

I had to make up for the mess I had made, and would do whatever it takes.

Changing Your Neural Pathways

The interesting thing about the brain is that it is constantly changing, adapting, rewiring itself based on the feedback it gets from the experiences we have.

And if you know how, you can hack it - reprogram it - fairly quickly and easily. Because of the way it operates, your brain doesn't know the difference between a *real* experience and an *intensely imagined* experience. So by tricking it with some NLP techniques we can blur old patterns (like gambling) and install new ones that serve us much better.

Your brain is hardwired by evolution to avoid PAIN and move toward PLEASURE, and we're going to tap into this to rewire our addicted brain.

But Before We Begin..

For this to work for you, you <u>must</u> first adopt these two beliefs:

1. **Change IS possible.**
To make this a long-lasting change you must know you *can* change anything right *now*, in an instant, because it is not the change itself that takes time. Problems can be created quickly - your first gambling experiences imprinted themselves on your brain instantly – so why not solutions? What are the consequences of *not* changing and what are the benefits of creating lasting change?

2. **YOU are responsible for making it change.**
It's your mind and *YOUR* responsibility for its change, and only you. Whatever happens *you* must take responsibility. Remember that being responsible simply means the ability to respond. What will it feel like if gambling is finally behind you, and you are free to live your life?

NAC Step 1:
Decide what you really want, and what is preventing you from having it right now.

Most people tend to focus on what they *don't* want, instead of what they *do* want. But did you know that your subconscious mind (85% of your whole brain) is literal and doesn't understand negatives?

For example, if you say "*I don't want to eat chocolate*", your brain hears the instruction: '*eat chocolate*'. The same is true for gambling. By saying "*I don't want to gamble*" or don't want to have a bet, your subconscious brain hears: '*want gamble*'.

This is partly because of the way the subconscious stores and retrieves information, and partly because of your R.A.S. – Reticular Activation System. Basically your brain goes off to find whatever it thinks is important to you. So for example, when you buy a silver car, you suddenly notice all the other silver cars on the road. Your RAS takes basic instruction and looks for more instances of it.

So rather than figuring out what you *don't* want, it's massively important to specify & instruct your brain about what you DO want: a better relationship, more money, savings in the bank, a bigger house, more self-respect, to be happier and more content, etc. Your brain can then start to work out where those things are and what it has to do to get them for you.

Once you've defined what you DO want, ask yourself: *"What are my limiting beliefs?"*

These might be things like:

- I'm not good enough..
- No-one will put up with me
- I always screw things up..
- I have no self control..
- I don't have enough..
- I'll never make it..
- It's better not to try new things..
- There's no point even trying..
- ...

Write down some of *your* top handicapping beliefs, you'll need them in the next step.

NAC Step 2:
Get Leverage - Associate Massive Pain to *not* changing NOW, and Massive Pleasure to Changing NOW.

As Human Beings we are all on the same journey: *Moving towards Pleasure and away from Pain.* We seek out security, fun, money, relationships, rewards (all under the Pleasure heading). And try to avoid loneliness, isolation, insecurity (all different types of Pain).

In order to change we need to change our *Shoulds* into *MUSTS.* The only way to do that is create a sense of urgency that is so *intense* that you can't wait any longer to put it off. To create change we have to realise that it is not the question of *can* we do it, it is the absolute intention that we WILL do it because we MUST do it.

To associate pain, you can ask yourself: *What does this cost me if I don't make this shift now?*

You have to make this pain so real, so intense, that you feel it emotionally and physically. A great way to do this is with the **Dickensian exercise** by Tony Robbins which will get you fired up and hopefully crying your eyes out. For this to have an effect, make sure you *feel* the pain of not changing. You'll know you're doing this exercise right when tears are literally running down your face! That's the emotional intensity your brain takes as an instruction to build new neural pathways, as it can feel it's important to you.

The Dickensian Process

If you need help associating massive pain to change, I highly recommend this exercise which gets its name from Charles Dickens' *A Christmas Carol* in which Scrooge is visited by ghosts showing him his past, present, and future.

You'll need a quiet space for 20 minutes and (if you do it right) a box of tissues. As you do this, *See it, Hear, it, FEEL it.*

In this process you're forced to examine limiting beliefs — say, your top two or three handicapping beliefs — across each tense. Then, take a look at each belief in depth and answer the following questions:

*"What has this belief cost me in the **PAST**, and what has it cost people I've loved in the past? What have I lost because of this belief? See it, hear it, feel it."*

*"What is this belief costing me and people I care about in the **PRESENT**? See it, hear it, feel it."*

*"What will this belief cost me and people I care about **1, 3, 5, and 10 YEARS FROM NOW**? See it, hear it, feel it."*

Only once you have associated massive pain to not changing, can you then start using pleasure associating questions to help you link those positive feelings to the idea of changing, like these:

If I DO change, how will I feel about myself?
What will I accomplish?
How happy will I be?

The trick is to get a *LOT* of reasons – massive, real reasons to make the change *now*, immediately. Every long-lasting change is first made in your subconscious mind.

[Long before I found out about NAC, I gave up smoking on my own. I had chain smoked 20 a day for 10 years, smoking an extra 20 on the night if I went out. In that decade there wasn't a single day in that I didn't start the day without a cigarette. If I ran out I would start to panic and physically shake. I would rollup used fag ends into a cigarette paper just to have something to smoke. I was without a doubt completely addicted to smoking.

When I finally decided it was time to quit, I knew it would be hard. So I wrote down a list on a piece of paper of 3 or 4 things that I wanted to gain from quitting. I started with better health, saving money, whiter teeth and clearer lungs. I then listed some more things to do with friends and family. I allowed myself to visualise and feel the outcomes if I didn't change, and how I would feel if I did change. I ended up with 2 sides of over **50 reasons** of how my life would be better if I was finally free of smoking. I kept that list in my back pocket for 6 months. The first week was incredibly tough, but I kept pulling out the piece of paper and reminding myself of why I was doing it until the craving had passed. Within a week the cravings got less and after a month I hardly missed it at all. I have never smoked again to this day.]

NAC Step 3:
Interrupt the Limiting Pattern

Ever seen a fly trying to escape from a room, bumping into the window again and again, and again? If only he came away from the window and had a look around the room, he would see there were other ways out. He needs to change his approach.

Let's say you had a music CD which played fine. If you picked it up and put a *massive deep scratch* in it, do you think it would still play? Probably not.

Or perhaps you have a movie clip stored on your hard drive. If you altered the file by changing its name, changed the file association of the programme that opens it, and then encrypted it - do you think it would still play? Doubtful, it would be too messed up.

Well you can do the same thing with subconscious memories which underpin our current behaviour. All our images, memories and the feelings we associate with them are stored in the brain (our hard drive). At the point of trigger or recall they are located, summoned up, stitched together, and play in our head like a video on demand. We even *feel* the feelings associated with them. But what if those reference memories were scrambled, interfered with. Would our internal movie still play?

And what if that movie was about our wonderful relationship with gambling. Could we mess that up, so our subconscious that directs so much of our behaviour can no longer reference the big buzz and the associated feelings? Our current behaviour *depends* on these references, just like a building relies on its foundations. But what if they weren't there? Could we really update and overwrite our gambling memories, so that they could no longer influence our subconscious and conscious mind?

How to Scramble a Memory

Here is a quick Neurolinguistic Programming (NLP) visualisation exercise for you to have a go at. Crazy as it seems, this stuff WORKS as it actually overwrites existing memories.

We're going to have a go at wrecking the memory of your best ever gambling win. To get results, make all the images large and clear in your mind, larger than life.

- Close your eyes and imagine the scene of your first ever big significant win. *See* what you saw, *hear* what you heard, really *feel* what you really felt. Don't worry if this freaks you out – it means you are reliving it again, which is what we're going for.

- See the scene running normally with yourself smiling and everyone patting you on the back.

- Now run it in reverse, from end to start.

- Now run it forwards, but this time at double speed.

- Change your own character to a clumsy cartoon character like Goofy, or a famous person you don't like.

- Run it again, but instead of winning a bunch of clowns come out with LOSER written on balloons and flags.

- After finishing you're now in the circus ring, being shot out of a canon.

- Nobody is laughing or applauding as nobody is impressed by your gambling, not even you.

- The last step is to make the whole scene go Black and White, draining all the colour from it. Then move away into the distance. Visualise it getting further and further away until it's tiny and you can hardly see it.

Repeat this process x5 times continuously for around 20 minutes until you are really tired of it. Then do it again tomorrow, using a different memory of gambling. If you do this as described each day for a week, you'll struggle to even remember your first win and we will have shaken your subconscious belief that gambling is making you successful.

The above is an example of a pattern interrupt. Feel free to tailor it to what you want in order to really mess up your best gambling memories. Change elements of it and make the old memory really exaggerated, silly and pathetic. Make everything big and colourful to start with, then black and white and really small to finish with.

It works – but only if you do it!

NAC Step 4:
Create a New, Empowering Alternative

With the old pattern scrambled you're now ready for the fourth step – to create a new empowering alternative. Most people fail to establish lasting change because they have nothing to replace the old pattern. Consequently their change is only temporary, and sooner or later they will get back to their old pattern.

And you must find an empowering alternative that retains the useful aspects of the old one. Every behaviour must have its own positive impacts; otherwise you would not be doing it. For instance, gambling might have de-stressed you, so it's important that your new replacement behaviour also de-stresses you. If it doesn't you'll just end up reverting back to the old behaviour, understand? Lots of people fail this way.

It's also important to **celebrate the new behaviour**. Once a week go for a drink or cheap meal if you can afford one, or cook a meal, or subscribe to the gym with the money you're saving, or go to the cinema... you get the idea. If money is extremely tight then simply go for a walk or run. Climb a hill and celebrate like Rocky. Demonstrate to your brain that the new way is beneficial and enjoyable, and something you should be proud of.

Note that it's extremely important that you consciously choose a new, empowering alternative. Otherwise your subconscious will automatically make the choice for you.

A smoker for example who quits might end switching to food, as putting something in their mouth temporarily stops the craving. But then they gain weight and have another problem: low self-esteem. However had they thought about the replacement activity and instead taken up a dance class with the money saved, then they would have made a healthier choice. And the endorphins released in their brains by the exercise would have made them feel just as good as smoking (if not better).

They would not just have given something up, they would have *gained something* potentially a lot more valuable: increased fitness and higher self-esteem, and made new friends too.

NAC Step 5:
Condition the new pattern until it's consistent

Our brains can't tell the difference between something we vividly imagine and something that we actually experienced. So the surest and most effective way to change your neural associations is simply to mentally rehearse it over and over in your mind, until it is embedded.

Reinforce the pattern with small rewards as often as you can. Give that new behaviour a pat on the back and let it know it's here to stay – by doing so you are reinforcing it and making damn sure it *does* stay.

If you struggle at any point in this process, don't beat yourself up. Just go back, get yourself even more leverage and start again. And this time when you visualise things, don't just go through the motions - really <u>FEEL</u> the emotion which helps establish the neural pathways rapidly and embed the new thinking stronger than before.

Make this a daily practice and you will soon have the results that you want.

So to recap:

1. **Decide what you really want** and what's preventing you from having it now.

2. **Get leverage:** Associate massive PAIN to not changing now, and massive PLEASURE to the experience of changing NOW.

3. **Interrupt the limiting pattern.**

4. **Create a new, empowering alternative**.

5. **Condition the new pattern until it's consistent.**

You can test the pattern using the checklist on the next page.

Test the New Pattern

1. Make certain PAIN is fully associated with the old pattern.

When you think of your old behaviour or feelings, do you picture and feel things that are painful now instead of pleasurable?

2. Make certain PLEASURE is fully associated with the new pattern.

When you think of your new behaviour or feelings, do you picture and feel things that are pleasurable now instead of painful?

3. Check the new pattern aligned with your values beliefs and rules.

Is the new behaviour or feeling consistent with the values, beliefs, and rules in your life?

4. Make sure the benefits of the old pattern have been maintained.

Will the new behaviour or feeling still allow you to get the benefits and feelings of pleasure that you used to get from the old pattern?

5. Future pace – Imagine yourself behaving in this new way in the future.

Imagine the thing that would've triggered you to adopt the old pattern. Feel certain that you can use your new pattern instead of the old one.

* * *

How Does Neuro-Associative Conditioning (NAC) Work?

NAC has its roots in NLP (Neurolinguistic Programming) which has been around for decades. NLP has been used by hundreds of thousands of therapists in millions of sessions worldwide to update clients' neural patterns.

NAC is Tony Robbins' own brand of NLP, which in many ways is much more effective. Tony uses NAC to bring about change to around 5 million people a year through his seminars and digital courses.

Remember YOU have to put the work in, and you have to *feel* the change and the pain of not changing. Don't waste your time just going through the motions – BE HONEST AND FEEL IT.

And as before, if you are going to do this you still need to build out the various aspects of your life. You will have a large *"gambling shaped gap"* which must be filled with all the old things you have been neglecting, and some new things too.

Start living a Multicentred way of life - some work, some friends & family time, some partner time, time for your kids, some sports or exercise, and some hobbies or interests. And some time when you help others and it's not just about you. Be a part of the community or other group.

Your goal shouldn't be to *not* do something, but to DO and CREATE something.

To move away from the Pain and Powerlessness of Addiction towards a Happy, Productive, Fulfilling Life.

Chapter 24
Diet & Exercise

I can't overstate the importance of Exercise in mental health recovery. If you don't currently do anything then the hardest part is the decision to get started. But if you can get yourself to start or do more, the benefits are huge (from a variety of perspectives).

Eating the right diet and doing the right kind of exercise can also massively reduce withdrawal symptoms. Personally I found these to be a great way to manage my own. Every time I would get thoughts of gambling or a bad urge, I would drop down and do 20 press-ups, go out for a walk or a run, or hit the gym. And I really do mean 'hit' – those workouts really helped me get it out of my system!

Over the years I've known people who used exercise *solely* as their recovery programme.

And did you know that the best natural way to boost our old friends Serotonin, Noradrenaline, Dopamine and Endorphins is *cardiovascular exercise*?

Any health concerns check with your GP first of course before using anything in this section.

Making Your Craving Work <u>FOR</u> You

Rather than running from the craving or trying to distract from it or dial it down, some people I know have actually used their craving to *help* them. After all, the only difference between a passion and an addiction is <u>who is in control</u> – the person or the behaviour.

Some people think that it's not the feeling of desire that's bad, it's what it's pointing at. And when you take that same feeling/intensity and point it towards your future, and your desire better health, better success, and desire to be better to the people around you, then you will be making progress.

This certainly works when you apply it to exercise as there are many mental and physical benefits. There's a lot of Addicts running and in spin classes right now shouting "BRING IT ON!" in their heads, and turning UP the urge while directing it towards their Health & Wellbeing.

And each time they do something different, the old unused pathways shrink back and get weaker, while the new empowering ones become stronger and more established.

MENTAL

Exercise naturally creates Endorphins, those feel good chemicals in your brain. When we're gambling or thinking about gambling, we are seeking that same feel-good feeling.

Recent research has revealed that exercise also generates something similar to cannabis in your brain! Known as *'runners high'* the body releases *Endocannabinoids*, self-produced chemicals similar to those found in marijuana. Yes, your brain makes its own weed.

A recent study by researchers at the University of Heidelberg medical school in Germany found that mice showed elevated levels of both Endorphins and Endocannabinoids after running, an activity they engage in for fun. The researchers also observed that mice were less sensitive to pain, less anxious and more tranquil after running, shown by their willingness to spend time in lighted areas of their cages rather than retreating to dark corners. Typically the mice displayed runners' high after 5km distance, which is thought to be same for humans.

When the team used drugs to block the animals' endocannabinoid receptors, the mice were no longer relaxed after running, proving to be just as anxious as before their runs and very sensitive to pain. Blocking opioid receptors, on the other hand, didn't affect the creatures' post-run tranquillity.

So thanks to Mother Nature we already have a built-in pain management system, triggered by exercise – make good use of it!

PHYSICAL

If you've been compulsive gambling then you have been neglecting your body. Over 25 years of working with Gambling Addicts, I rarely find a Gambler that is fit and healthy. And the deep stress within the body is evident: facial stress, twitching hands and feet, and a hunched posture. Often lack of eye contact reflecting the inner self-esteem. Gamblers don't smile easily and naturally without putting on an act.

And let's not even get into the effect of gambling on the heart and blood pressure! You simply cannot put that much Cortisol and Adrenaline through your body on a regular basis, combined with poor quality sleep over a sustained period of time, without expecting consequences. I myself had to undergo heart surgery recently. And this was a quarter of a century after my last bet! Everything catches up with you eventually.

Exercise however changes all this. Within a week of doing some kind of light to moderate exercise your posture will become more upright, cardiovascular health will start to improve, and the stress will start to leave your body. You will feel better about yourself too.

EMOTIONAL

Exercise is proven to help lift Anxiety and Depression (common problems for Problem Gamblers) especially in the early weeks. Let's face it, life isn't exactly rosy.

But rather than turning to Antidepressants, why not try a natural remedy first – exercise.

Endorphins are the body's very own natural antidepressant. But exercise also releases other neurotransmitters like *Serotonin*, which lift mood. Serotonin is a chemical that is lowered during depressed mental states. Brain-Derived Neurotrophic Factor (BDNF), a chemical that promotes brain health and memory, is also reduced in depression, and exercise has been found to elevate levels of this neurotransmitter too.

So exercise is a quick and fairly immediate way to manage your mood, and could be a great alternative to Antidepressants that doctors hand out too readily.

SLEEP

Endorphins improve sleep, a precious commodity when you're caught in the vicious cycle of a gambling addiction. And sleep provides the brain with the necessary downtime to process the day's learning, repair the body, and recoup energy for the next day.

So if you want to start sleeping properly again as well as get a better perspective on your life, start exercising again. It's amazing how different the world seems when you've had a decent night's sleep.

The Key Benefits of Exercise

- Reduce Stress
- Ward off Anxiety and Depression
- Boost Self Esteem
- Improve Sleep
- Strengthen your heart
- Increase energy levels
- Lower blood pressure
- Improves muscle tone and strength
- Strengthen and build bones
- Help reduce body fat
- Look fit and healthy

How to Get Started

Don't overthink this! Just start TODAY from where you are, with what you've got. Just like making your bed in the Morning Routine, get something quick and simple done and then you have *already* started.

You don't need a gym membership or all the gear - just get outdoors and put one foot in front of the other. Start with a 10-minute walk at a pace that you are comfortable with and build it up from there. Obviously if you've got any health complaints then check with your medical practitioner first.

If possible, rope someone else into exercising with you. This will help keep it going after the initial burst of motivation has gone. Have a chat as you walk or go the gym / fitness class together. Do some light weights and gradually increase to build up muscle tone (which will help increase bone density and help burn more calories too).

Or if you're without friends and completely broke there's a stack of great free fitness videos on YouTube, Amazon, and other platforms that you can work out to. Jump around in the kitchen or living room and get your heart rate up a little. Just make the decision and start NOW – no more putting it off.

And after the first week start setting some goals. Visualise how fit you would like to become within say 12 months, and what you would like to weigh and like to look like. Visualise and feel this in your body every morning – it's yet another thing that you are moving towards.

Make it easy on yourself by scheduling your exercise within your Daily Programme! It can become a vital pillar in your new life.

Get Generating Neurotransmitters!

Remember that the best natural way to boost Serotonin, Noradrenaline, Dopamine and Endorphins all together is *cardiovascular exercise.*

Start gentle, but when you're up to it move towards HIIT (*High Intensity Interval Training*) where you will work to 80-90% of your work/heart rate for short 1-minute bursts, resting 30 seconds between bursts. Spin classes are great for this.

A few 20-minute HIIT sessions x3 times a week will get you all the Neurotransmitters you need! And you'll look good too. Obviously check with your doctor first if you have any concerns, and build up to your maximum.

* * *

How Does Exercise Work as a Recovery Technique?

Exercise generates all the Neurotransmitters that you normally get from gambling, and improves your self-esteem too. Your current brain-balance expects a lot of neurotransmitters on a daily basis, which it will crave if it doesn't get them. So replacing them with ones generated by exercise is a smart move, resulting in less urges and withdrawal symptoms.

Exercise can also be a social activity getting you out and about with people, which is mentally healthy for loners like us. Great activity to do with others, especially outdoors in nature rather than inside looking at screen or tied to a machine.

And seeing visual results in your fitness as it improves gives you tangible confidence that gambling is behind you, and the new "You 2.0" is being born.

Usual Reminder: YOU have to put the work in, and YOU have to make change happen. So schedule it in your Daily Programme to make sure it happens.

And as before, exercise is great but you still need to build out the various aspects of your life! You will have a large *"gambling shaped gap"* which must be filled with all the old things you have been neglecting, and some new things too.

Make this part of your commitment to start living a more Multicentred way of life - some work, some friends & family time, some partner time, time for your kids, some sports or exercise, and some hobbies or interests. And some time when you help others and it's not just about you. Be a part of the community or other group.

Your goal shouldn't be negative - to *not* do something - but to DO and CREATE something.

Leave the Pain of Addiction behind and move towards a Happy, Balanced, Healthy Life.

Next up: Diet.

Diet

Gamblers often depend on fast food, sugar, caffeine, sex, nicotine and alcohol to get them through the day and night. I myself used to exist this way when I was gambling, but wasn't particularly bothered as I had convinced myself that I wasn't go to live past 30 (seriously). A typical ADD trait by the way – the inability to comprehend or prepare for the future.

But as I approached 29 my reckless behaviour caught up with me and I was forced to do something about it. Looking back, that was actually one of the most important times of my life as I was at a crossroads – an opportunity for me to take a different path.

But even at the age of 7, well before my gambling established itself, I was a junior junkie. I was having a cup to tea with 6 spoons of sugar in it - so much sugar that it wouldn't even dissolve properly. I would dunk at least 4 biscuits in it as well. And after I drank it I would feel high, alive, in touch. Then I'd get the sweats as my brain and my body became overloaded trying to process the sugar overload. And 20 minutes later I would be exhausted in a sugar *slump* after the high had gone. So, only one thing to do – have another one! 45 years later I recognise this as another typical ADD behaviour, trying to wake up the brain, seeking *the warm hug of a mother*.

Having several cups of sugar a day (sorry, tea) I was up and down like a yo-yo for years, followed by the same yo-yo pattern with gambling, alcohol, chocolate, sex, fizzy drinks, gaming and smoking. Any way possible to change my mood, to bring me up a level and keep me there.

But over the years I have learned there is a much easier way to elevate and stabilize your mood, through the fuel that you put into your body.

And if you are serious about tacking your gambling problem, you'll find it much easier if you avoid the highs and lows that a poor diet will give you.

Later in this section I've provided guidance on specific foods and supplements that will help keep your Dopamine and Serotonin levels topped up naturally, which will reduce your depression and cravings to Gamble.

The Importance of Regular Meals

Try to eat 3-4 small meals a day, spread out at regular intervals through the day. This helps regulate blood sugar so that you are never really starving, and therefore not experiencing low blood sugar and the body's natural anxiety associated with this.

Always eat breakfast, ideally containing 30g of protein that will keep you full for longer. Try porridge or oats with added protein powder, or some avocado and eggs on toast with a little spinach which will set you up for the day.

Sugary cereals with little protein value are a bad idea, and won't keep you full for very long.

If you don't already know, the gut is sometimes referred to as *"the second brain"* (or the Enteric Nervous Systems to give it the proper name) and contains some 500 million neurons! **95%** of the body's Serotonin is actually found in the bowels. Your 'second brain' is connected to your main brain (which is why we get butterflies, nervous tummy, etc) and treating one badly will have an effect on the other.

It's amazing how often an urge to Gamble actually started in our gut as the simple need to eat something! This leads to anxiety and a feeling of restlessness & irritability, which resulted in the self-medication of gambling.

The Importance of Drinking Water

Most Gamblers are very poor at hydration. But did you know that:

1. Dehydration Affects your Mood

A number of studies have identified a link between dehydration and mood disturbances. In a 2012 study, researchers at the University of Connecticut induced dehydration in healthy young women through either exercise or exercise plus a diuretic, and assessed its effects on mood state. Dehydration was found to result in a measurable increase in *total mood disturbance*.

2. Dehydration Reduces your Cognitive and Motor skills

We all know not to drive under the influence of alcohol, but a 2015 Loughborough University study indicated that we should also avoid *driving* dehydrated. Volunteers committed a significantly greater number of errors such as lane drifting and late braking in a two-hour driving simulation when they did it dehydrated. In fact, their performance was just as poor as that of people who complete similar tests while at the legal limit for blood alcohol content. The likely reason is that dehydration reduces concentration and reaction time. If we are attempting to get our brain into Recovery then we need to hydrate.

3. Dehydration makes you More Sensitive to Pain

Dehydration results in increased pain sensitivity, as according to a 2014 study by Japanese researchers. Volunteers immersed an arm in cold water to test their pain sensitivity while having their brains scanned. They reported a lower pain threshold (i.e. they felt pain sooner) when they performed this test in a dehydrated state. These subjective reports were accompanied by increased activity in brain areas involved in the experience of pain.

4. Dehydration affects your Memory

And if all of that wasn't enough, dehydration has also been found to negatively impact memory. Researchers at Ohio University measured hydration status in a group of 21 older women and also had them complete tests of declarative and working memory. A strong link between hydration status and memory skills was found, with the most dehydrated subjects performing most poorly on the tests. This effect was partly mediated by blood pressure.

Your brain is mostly water - no wonder it works better when it's properly hydrated!

So if you're in recovery, *drink water* – at least 8 decent sized glasses a day, throughout the day. Good hydration will help reduce your withdrawal symptoms and help regulate your mood.

General Healthy Eating Tips for a Stable Mood

Just like we are going to get balance into our lives, we are going to try the same with our diet. Some basics are:

1. Divide your plate into thirds, so you have one third protein, one third carbohydrates, and one third vegetables/legumes/fruit

2. Meat eaters, stick more to white meat and fish than red meat

3. Cut back on greasy, fatty foods as they will give you that slump that you are looking to avoid

4. Reduce your number of takeaways a week, instead going to a supermarket to handpick your food. Look at the labels, and learn about what is good for you and what is not. Reduce the sugars in particular and choose food that is higher in protein which will keep you fuller for longer (therefore with more stable blood sugar and less body anxiety).

Specific Mood-Boosting Foods

Gambling makes us feel good by manipulating brain chemicals called neurotransmitters. That's what's *really* happening when you press those buttons – getting your drugs just like those rats in the cages.

But why rely on Gambling to give you an artificial high, when you can get the exact same neurotransmitters from natural, healthy food? Lot cheaper and less stressful too!

Avocado   *Oleic Acid Gives You Brainpower*

Avocados are power foods that contain *healthy fats* your brain needs in order to run smoothly. Three quarters of the calories of an avocado are from fat, mostly monounsaturated fat, in the form of oleic acid. An average avocado also contains 4 grams of protein, higher than other fruits, and is filled with vitamin K, different kinds of vitamin B (B9, B6, and B5), vitamin C, and vitamin E12. Finally, they are low in sugar and high in dietary fibre, containing about 11 grams each. Keeps you full for longer.

Dark Leafy Greens	*A Nutrient-Dense Inflammation Fighter* Dark, leafy greens, Spinach, Kale, Swiss Chard. Powerful immune-boosting and anticancer effects. Leafy greens fight against all kinds of inflammation, and according to a study published in March 2015 in JAMA Psychiatry, severe depression has been linked with *brain inflammation.* Leafy greens are especially important because they contain plenty of vitamins A, C, E, and K, minerals, and phytochemicals.
Walnuts	*Rich in Mood-Boosting Omega-3 Fatty Acids* Walnuts are one of the richest plant sources of omega-3 fatty acids, and many studies have demonstrated how omega-3 fatty acids support brain function and *reduce depression* symptoms.
Berries	*Full of Cell-Repairing Antioxidants* Blueberries, raspberries, strawberries, and blackberries are some of the highest *antioxidant* foods available to us. Keep

some in and try them in porridge or on cereal. In a study published in the Journal of Nutritional and Environmental Medicine, patients were treated for two years with antioxidants or placebos. After two years those who were treated with antioxidants had a *significantly lower depression* score. You might think of antioxidants as 'DNA repairmen', going around fixing your cells and preventing them from getting cancer and other illnesses.

Mushrooms *Lowering Blood Sugar*

Mushrooms are good for your mental health as firstly, their chemical properties oppose Insulin, which *helps lower blood sugar* levels, evening out your mood. And secondly they act like a *probiotic* in that they promote healthy gut bacteria. And since the nerve cells in our gut manufacture 80 to 90 percent of our body's Serotonin — the neurotransmitter that keeps us calm — we can't afford to not pay attention to our intestinal health.

Tomatoes   *The Depression Ninjas*

At least six baby tomatoes a day in a salad each day helps because tomatoes contain lots of folic acid and alpha-lipoic acid, both great at fighting depression. According to research published in the Journal of Psychiatry and Neuroscience, many studies show an elevated incidence of folate deficiency in patients with depression. In most of the studies, about one-third of depression patients were deficient in folate.

Folic acid can prevent an excess of *homocysteine* — which in turn restricts the production of important Neurotransmitters like serotonin, dopamine, and norepinephrine — from forming in the body.

Onions   *Contain Cancer-Fighting Allium*

Onions and all Allium veg (garlic, leeks, chives, shallots, and spring onions) have all been associated with a decreased risk of several cancers. If you consider the relationship between your digestive tract and your brain, it is understandable why a food that can prevent cancers of the gut can also benefit your mood.

Beans   *Satisfyingly High in Mood-Stabilizing Fibre*

Beans work as anti-diabetes and weight-loss foods. They are good for mood because the body digests them slowly, which stabilizes blood sugar levels. Any food that assists you in balancing your blood sugar levels is your friend.

Apples   *Ripe with Antioxidants and Fibre*

Like berries, apples are high in antioxidants which can help to prevent and repair oxidation damage and inflammation on the cellular level. They are also full of soluble fibre, which balances blood sugar swings.

Seeds *Small but Mighty Sources of Omega-3's*

Seeds are a great replacement for convenience comfort foods. Flaxseeds, hemp seeds, and chia seeds are especially good for your mood because they are rich in omega-3 fatty acids. The fat in seeds may also increase the absorption of protective nutrients in vegetables eaten at the same meal.

The Dopamine Diet

The Dopamine Diet is billed as the weight loss regime that boosts mood too. It is all about increasing levels of the 'happy hormone' dopamine in the brain at the same time as shedding pounds. Certain celebrities such as TV chef Tom Kerridge have boosted this diet's popularity in recent years and has a book out on it (called The Dopamine Diet).

There are several different versions of the diet, but all are based around foods that are thought to boost dopamine including:

- Dairy foods such as milk, cheese and yogurt
- Unprocessed meats such as beef, chicken and turkey
- Omega-3 rich fish such as salmon and mackerel
- Eggs
- Fruit and vegetables, in particular bananas
- Nuts such as almonds and walnuts
- Dark chocolate

The Serotonin Diet

Serotonin is a chemical messenger that's believed to act as a mood stabiliser. It's said to help produce healthy sleeping patterns as well as boost your mood. Studies show that serotonin levels can have an effect on mood and behaviour, and the chemical is commonly linked to feeling good and living longer.

Serotonin isn't found in foods, but *Tryptophan* is. Foods high in protein, iron, riboflavin, and vitamin B-6 all tend to contain large amounts of this amino acid.

So, in order to increase your Serotonin levels naturally, you can try eating foods that contain tryptophan. It is known that tryptophan depletion is seen in those with mood disorders such as depression and anxiety.

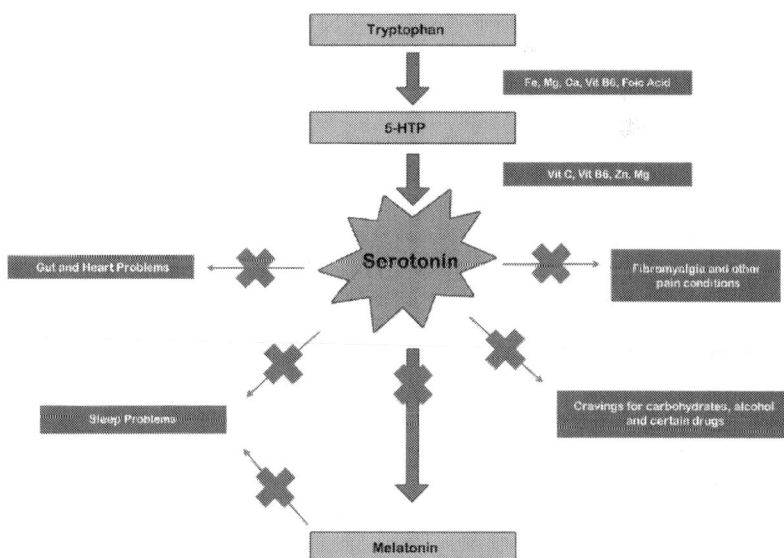

As you can see lack of Serotonin causes Gut and heart problems, Fibromyalgia and other pain conditions, disturbed sleep and cravings for alcohol, carbs and other things.

To get enough Serotonin into your brain and body, make sure the following are in your recovery diet:

Salmon   It's hard to go wrong with salmon, which is also rich in tryptophan. Why not combine it with eggs and milk to make a smoked salmon frittata! Salmon also has other nutritional benefits like helping balance cholesterol, lowering blood pressure, and being a source of omega-3 fatty acids.

Eggs   The protein in eggs can significantly boost your blood plasma levels of tryptophan, according to recent research. Include the yolks which are extremely rich in tryptophan and tyrosine, choline, biotin, omega-3 fatty acids, and other nutrients that are major contributors to the health benefits and antioxidant properties of eggs.

Turkey   Turkey is essentially stuffed tryptophan, and low in fat too.

Cheese   Cheese is another great source of tryptophan. You could make a mac and cheese that combines cheddar cheese with eggs and milk, good sources of tryptophan as well.

Tofu   Soy products are rich sources of tryptophan. You can substitute tofu for pretty much any protein, making it an excellent source of tryptophan for vegetarians and vegans. Some tofu is calcium-set, which provides a great calcium boost.

Pineapples Pineapples are a major source of bromelain, a protein that can reduce the side effects of chemotherapy as well as help suppress coughs, according to some research.

Nuts and Seeds	All nuts and seeds contain tryptophan, so pick and choose your favourites. Nuts and seeds are good sources of fibre, vitamins, and antioxidants. Studies show that eating a handful of nuts a day can lower your risk for cancer, heart disease, and respiratory problems. For dessert, try some no-bake peanut butter oatmeal cookies.

Other ways to Boost Serotonin

Food and supplements aren't the only ways to boost serotonin levels.

- **Exercise** - Regular exercise can have antidepressant effects
- **Sunshine** - Light therapy is a common remedy for seasonal depression. Research shows a clear relationship between being exposed to bright light and serotonin levels. To get better sleep, or to boost your mood, try a daily lunchtime walk outside!
- **Positivity** - Research shows that facing daily life and your interactions with others with a positive outlook can significantly boost your serotonin levels. Don't be a loner.
- **Gut bacteria** - Eat a high-fibre diet to fuel your healthy gut bacteria, which new research shows play a role in serotonin levels through the gut-brain relationship. Taking a Probiotics supplement may also help keep your gut optimal.

Five Neurotransmitter Supplements

There are supplements available that can lift your mood naturally. Try them one at a time (not all at once!) and check first with your GP that they will not conflict with any other medication you are on. Do <u>not</u> take some of these if you are already on antidepressants.

Magnesium	Magnesium is involved in a range of vital functions of the brain of the cellular level, but the high stress caused by gambling depletes magnesium.
	Importantly magnesium is a key factor in the production of serotonin along with other vitamins such as folate.
Alpha-lipoic Acid	Alpha-lipoic acid is worth taking as a supplement as it helps the body convert glucose into energy, and therefore *stabilizes mood*.

St. John's Wort (Hypericum)	The king of natural antidepressants. No side effects like some drug-based antidepressants, but slower to get started before they get started. But less likely to be given up due to side effects.

Good at reducing Cortisol, before stress and depression set in.

Consistently increases levels of Serotonin, Noradrenaline and Dopamine in the brain (Serotonin most effectively, providing a feeling of calm). |
| **Curcumin** (Curcuma Longa) | Curcumin is the miraculous natural phenolic substance extracted from the popular spice Turmeric and is being research for everything from Alzheimer's to depression.

Curcumin also indirectly helps normalise serotonin levels by increasing levels of BDNF (Brain Derived Neutrophic Factor) your brain's "fertiliser". Increasing levels of BDNF theoretically accelerates the healing process which would include your serotonergic system. |

Rhodiola Rosea

Rhodiola is a herbal supplement most commonly used for increasing energy, endurance, strength, and mental capacity. It is also used as a so-called "adaptogen" to help the body adapt to and resist physical, chemical, and environmental stress.

Used for decades in Russia, Asia and Alaska to treat nervous disorders including stress anxiety and depression.

Rhodiola increases levels of serotonin which helps you sleep. So if you are anxious, depressed or highly stressed this should help. It is affectively a natural antidepressant.

* * *

How Does Diet Work as a Recovery Technique?

Food is fuel for the body, but we often forget that it is also fuel for the *mind*. Your brain in fact uses 20% of your daily calorie intake.

We know from our earlier chemistry lesson that the brain produces its own feel good chemicals (neurotransmitters) like Dopamine and Serotonin.

And when we gamble we are really just trying to *control* how much of those chemicals are produced in our brain - in order to avoid, cope with, or escape our *real* problem (just like those Rats in the cages that were trying to escape their stress and isolation).

Eating the right foods will give you the energy to exercise (which in itself will help you generate neurotransmitters) and also help keep your neurotransmitter levels topped up throughout the day. Not only a more natural way to do it, but a lot cheaper and less stressful than gambling!

And your body will thank you for it. With more Serotonin in your diet you will sleep better, giving your body a better chance of recharging itself and your brain the opportunity to rewire new memories and behaviours.

Gambling has most likely taken *years* off your life, perhaps it's time to put some back? If not for yourself, for the others in your life. Or for the person you hope to meet and the children you might one day have.

Chapter 25
Join a Tribe

I get it. We feel ashamed and embarrassed by our inability to control what everyone else seems to be able to. We want to sort it out on our own – I was exactly like that.

But we also know that we lack the tools and know-how to sort it or things wouldn't have got to this stage. That is one of the reasons I decided to write this book, to help people bridge the gap.

With the many Gambling Addicts I have known over the years, I'd have to be an idiot to miss why some people manage to free themselves of this addiction and others don't. I have observed that there are 2 essential conditions necessary for someone to overcome this problem.

They are:

1. ACCEPTANCE
2. TALKING

Firstly, it is impossible to overcome a problem if you are not willing to accept that you even have a problem.

Secondly if you avoid talking about the problem openly and <u>honestly</u> to at least *one* other human being, then you are still in denial at some level about accepting that you even have a problem (which takes us back to Acceptance).

If what I have just said brings out a *"Whoah, hold on there big fella..."* response in you, then let me tell you why it might be a smart move to part of a Recovery Tribe.

Short History of Tribes

Apes, humans, and all mammals have always existed in small collectives, or Tribes. This group would hunt together, sleep together, and protect each other. Without the tribe they were just individuals on their own - cold, hungry and vulnerable to predators. Loners didn't last long.

Tribes have their own ways of doing things and share knowledge from generation to generation. In ancient times and the middle ages, individuals within tribes performed different jobs like hunting, cooking, looking after the young, and so on. In fact you see this throughout the entire animal kingdom with ants, bees, and insects as it vastly improves the chances of their collective future survival.

The whole of civilisation has been built on tribes for generations, because it works. Many of us work for one (a Company) and relax with one (our Friends) and live in one (a Family).

Why Join a Self-Help Group?

When you want to break free of your Gambling Addiction, there are a lot of serious problems to address. It's definitely uphill for the first 3-6 months.

All gamblers think they have the answers to pretty much everything - that's how I was, and probably how you are too. Everything sounds fine when it's coming out of our mouths. It's only when our dreamworld comes crashing down or things don't work out as we planned, that we realise that we're not quite as smart as we think we are. Our consistently bad decisions have brought us to a desperate place.

As you tackle this you will be faced with questions and choices on a weekly basis, and decisions which threaten your survival (staying off gambling).

- What should I do and what shouldn't I do?

- Should I stay away from all forms of gambling or just the one that was a problem for me?

- How do I know what works and what doesn't?

- Am I the only one that feels this way?

- How should I tackle certain relationship problems or gambling-related financial problems?

- How do I know what to watch out for?

- What are the warning signs when I'm doing things wrong or going off course?

Over the first year you will face lots of challenges and, if you are doing it right, lots of changes. Those changes themselves bring their own challenges as it's all new. The addiction itself can be addressed reasonably quickly, but your life problems still exist until you sort them out. Given that we have been running away from them for a long time, we will probably need support. It also takes time to 'defrost' from the selfish numbness of gambling and become an outward facing, truthful person again.

I myself remember turning up my first GA meeting and telling one of the oldest members that I had no problems other than gambling! But as I realised over the next few months, I had in fact developed a whole lot of bad traits which I had no option but to address if I was to remain *off* gambling.

Opening Up

I attended the self-help group for some time and found that it helped me to start talking about my addiction. And as I heard the words coming out of my own mouth, I felt something change inside me.

Sitting in a room talking to other people in the same boat was like being in a room full of mirrors. Quite often I was blind to my own flaws and mistakes, but could see them clearly in others.

Advice & Accountability

When you first come off Gambling, you will need help from people you trust and good advice. And you will continue to need their help and advice in order to *stay* off it.

But we do not usually welcome such advice from partner, friends or family as we see it as interference. There is a lot of history, emotional baggage, that all parties carry with them.

However hearing the exact same advice from someone where there is no prior relationship can be readily accepted.

It is common for loved ones to refer the gambler to me and say something along the lines of "He won't listen to me, hopefully he will listen to you." That is usually the case.

And when we agree that we need to do something like contact a debtor, apply for a new job, implement the daily program, etc the simplest of follow up questions on *'how it's going'* can get a far more constructive response.

That question from the family might be seen as *interfering*, whereas the exact same question coming from someone else in recovery will get a simple answer without any of the noise we often make when we're uncomfortable or embarrassed.

The Hidden Benefit of Helping Others

Being part of recovery group can help you tell your story, and by doing so help others. Over the years I have found this to be one of THE most important elements of my own recovery: *Helping Others.* Every time I have supported another gambler just by listening or by offering some advice based on my own experience, it has not only helped them but helped *me.*

And every time I have tried to help someone else, I have further insulated myself against gambling. This is probably the **Number #1 reason** I have managed to stay off gambling for 25+ years. Trust me, it works.

Some of you will have already worked out that helping others met my own needs for *Growth* and *Contribution*, which in turn helped restore balance to my brain, my personality, and my life. **Golden Ticket!**

Overcoming Complacency

As I said at the very start of this book, the biggest battle you will face is your own gambling-wired mind - that inner voice of doubt and fear that constantly niggles: *"Do I really need to do that?"* And then the: *"I haven't gambled for two weeks - surely I must be cured by now?"* voice.

In my experience who better to point out that you're slacking off and heading for a fall, than someone like you?

They're probably the only person in the world that you are likely take advice from anyway.

What Gambling Support Tribes are there?

One of the oldest tribes is Gamblers Anonymous (GA) fellowship which was founded in 1957 following a chance meeting between two gamblers. They continued to meet up and talk about their problem with each other, and found it helped them both stay off gambling. After a while they borrowed the format and literature from AA (Alcoholics Anonymous) and GA was born. In GA Members follow the spiritual 'recovery programme'.

A new tribe called *GamHelp* has recently been established by the Author of this book. GamHelp is like an online version of GA, but more modern and without many of the aspects that put some people off trying GA. In GamHelp Members share what works for them, and the intention is to discuss and work through a lot of what you find in this book.

* * *

Chapter 26
Quick Daily Checklist
Use the following each day to stay on track.

BARRIERS IN PLACE?

- Money Management (someone looking after my money, just have access to what I need)
- Self-Excluded from Sites, Apps & Shops
- Gambling block software in place on all the phones, tablets and PC's that I have access to, which I cannot disable or uninstall and do not know the password for

ONE DAY AT A TIME.

- Get a Good Start!
  - Morning Routine (make bed, exercise, gratitude, do affirmations)
  - Go through the Daily Programme list I did last night
  - Do one of the mind exercises (eg. NAC)
- Follow my Daily Programme as closely as I can
- Stay Busy & Focussed on my Programme, hour at a time
- Keep Hydrated and Eat Little and Often (avoiding low blood sugar, keeping Dopamine & Serotonin up)
- Avoid Triggers (talking about gambling, walk other side of the street, change channel, etc)
- Do Periodic Mindfulness (few minutes here and there, especially if problems)
- Get some Exercise (walk, run, gym, cycle)
- At the end of the day finish by writing tomorrow's Daily Programme, and not too late to bed

GET BACK ON TRACK..

If I get an urge or things don't got to plan today, I won't stress or beat myself up - I will simply:

- Change my State
- Do 5 minutes of Mindfulness
- Talk to someone
- Do my affirmations (in head or out loud)
- Do some exercise (even 60 seconds will help)
- Switch to another task on my ToDo list

Change only happens
when I turn my SHOULDS into MUSTS.

"My **WHY** is: ...."

(write it down)

NEW
BEGINNINGS

Chapter 27
Review

The information in this book took me 10 years to experience, then a further 25 years to understand. After having lived through the problem myself and then a further quarter of a century helping others get over their problems, I'd have to be a fool not to recognise the common patterns and what works.

So I've done my best look at Gambling Addiction from various different angles, some of which I hope have struck a chord with you.

The first section, EXPERIENCE, should have helped you identify that you are problem gambler and need to take action. It should have opened your eyes to some of patterns that exist in your life and what's ahead if you don't you handle this thing now, once and for all. And *Immaturity* and unwillingness to grow up were flagged as common factors. So there. We all know that your inner child would rather avoid and run away from things than stand your ground, so your first challenge will be to get leverage on yourself. Find your WHY.

In SCIENCE we got behind the scenes to learn more about the brain, and how you use neurotransmitters to get yourself high, resulting in brain patterns that exactly resemble Crack Cocaine addicts. We also learned how a key decision-making part of our brain (the Prefrontal Cortex) shuts down when you're gambling, so you can't even decide to stop or walk away. You are literally *chained* to gambling. And while the PFC is offline, the brain centres for Stress, Anxiety, Fear and Dopamine are running the show. No wonder we feel like we've been mugged afterwards!

We also spent some time finding out about ADD and how it's common in gamblers (most of whom don't even know they have it) and how our *Prefrontal Cortex* and *Insular* are smaller too, resulting in an immature brain with immature behaviours. We discovered how our brain can establish new circuitry either the slow way (with *Repetition*) or the fast way (using *Emotion*). Most current gambling therapies focus on the slow ways, but like most gamblers I prefer the fast ways.

In CONNECTION we understood how rats living in a happy, social, stress-free environment didn't choose drugs, while those in an isolated caged environment chose to escape by zoning out every time. The same was true in the Vietnam War where 20% of the 3million soldiers out there were addicted to Heroin to get them through the horrors of war, but over 90% of returning addicts spontaneously gave up on being re-connected with their families and friends in their familiar, less stressed environment.

We learned about the SIX HUMAN NEEDS and found that if ONE thing meets any THREE of our needs for Certainty, Variety, Significance or Love/Connection then it's an Addiction. We also noted that *Connection* had come up yet again (a need which we were probably meeting by gambling) and that we hardly had any Growth or Contribution in our lives.

Then we got busy PREPARING to tackle the addiction, getting some leverage on ourselves by working out how much Time and Money gambling had cost us so far. We dived head first into putting temporary Safeguards in place, to make sure we couldn't just gamble the moment we felt the urge to. For insurance we enlisted a helper, tied up our money so it was less at risk, and put Gambling blocks and self-exclusions in place just in case. We now stood a much better chance of breaking the old cycle.

Our last piece of the preparation was to identify our TRIGGERS and think about how we might avoid them. We also considered what daily Events fired which specific Emotions, and prepared a list of things we could do if they came up, instead of reacting in the same way and self-medicating with gambling.

I introduced you to FIVE DAILY PROGRAMMES FOR A NEW LIFE to kickstart your recovery:

- Morning Routine
- Just for Today programme
- Growing Up Checklist
- Six Human Needs programme
- My Daily Programme

all of which will *definitely* help you restructure your day and your behaviour, to enable you to lead a happy, productive, multi-centred life free from gambling... *but only if you do them!* Incorporate elements of each into the Daily Programme and you'll have a real fighting chance of putting gambling behind you, and build a great life too.

Finally I gave you FIVE WAYS TO REPAIR AND UPGRADE YOUR MIND:

- Mindfulness
- State Management
- Neuro-Associative Conditioning
- Diet and Exercise
- Joining a Tribe

all of which will accelerate your progress massively if you practice them daily or several times a week. Your brain literally starts to rebuild itself *instantly* the moment you allow yourself to *FEEL* the emotion.

But you can't get fit by going to the gym once! Daily repetition is the key, especially in the early days. Train your brain and install heathy new habits.

* * *

Chapter 28
Restoring the Balance

On this journey we learned a lot about the brain and how we manipulate Dopamine to reward and escape ourselves. Gambling Addicts are without a doubt junkies, but not hooked on Dopamine (which you can't actually get physiologically addicted to anyway).

We learned about several factors including:

AN UNDERDEVELOPED BRAIN
IMMATURITY
ADD

NEUROTRANSMITTERS (DOPAMINE, SEROTONIN, ETC)
THE BRAIN (PREFRONTAL CORTEX, AMYGDALA, INSULAR)
STRESS

CONNECTION

So ... Why **DO** We Gamble Abnormally?

Here's my take on how all the pieces fit together. Actually I have two different ways of looking at it, both of which take us to the same conclusion.

#1 - Gambling is a BRAIN Disorder

We know that two key parts of a Problem Gambler's brain are underdeveloped and smaller than normal:

- The *Prefrontal Cortex* which enables us to make decisions and weigh up the consequences of our actions

- The *Insular* which stores our harmful experiences so we can avoid them in future.

The underdevelopment of these two key brain centres was most likely caused by either:

- **Developing Gambling Addiction Early in Life** (in our teenage years or early twenties) before our brain - specifically our prefrontal cortex - was fully formed, or

- **Undiagnosed ADD** which in itself could have been a result of:

  - Lack of attunement / attachment with the mother or primary care giver
  - An inherited genetic predisposition
  - Childhood trauma or adverse experience (PTSD)
  - Perceived trauma due to being a sensitive child

Whichever the original causes, we've got a smaller brain with an underdeveloped Prefrontal Cortex and Insular.

This kind of brain lends itself to selfish, **immature** behaviours with little concept of the future or the consequences of our current actions, than a larger fully formed, mature brain.

With this kind of brain, we go gambling with good intentions, to stick to our limits and quit while we're ahead. But somehow it all goes to SH*T every time.

It happens like this:

- Our body has an internal BALANCE (*homeostasis*) that has become used to the large amounts of Dopamine, Noradrenaline and other Neurotransmitters that Gambling generates. Without regular shots of them we feel *out of balance*, on edge, in withdrawal – under stimulated like nothing is exciting.

- We attempt to rectify this balance - and also treat our ADD and its defective **Prefrontal Cortex** - with a *bright, powerful stimulus* (GAMBLING) that engages several senses and all our attention. So when we are engaged by this stimulus, we feel like we are operating at full capacity, on all cylinders... because WE ARE. Gambling has kickstarted our lazy **Prefrontal Cortex** with **Noradrenaline** - now we feel alive, capable, fully engaged – and rewarded with **Dopamine**.

- But the only way for us to remain awake and engaged without interrupting our supply of **Noradrenaline** and **Dopamine** is to keep gambling. So we don't walk away when we're ahead, we continue. And we chase our losses when we're down. Meanwhile our **Stress** level builds up with massive amounts of **Cortisol**.

- Our **Prefrontal Cortex** becomes overloaded with **Cortisol** and shuts down, enabling us to risk far more money than we planned and play much longer that we planned.

- Control is handed off to our instinctive and emotional "chimp" brain, specifically the **Amygdala** and the **Hypothalamus**, which puts us on a scary rollercoaster of **Anger/Anxiety/Fear** and **Dopamine** where we're all over the place, taking more risks and betting quickly on anything. The emotional Amygdala panics and we experience brain freeze. Our Hypothalamus, the Janitor in charge of maintaining our brain's BALANCE (homeostasis), works hard to maintain the addicted brain state no matter how freaked out the Amygdala gets.

- Meanwhile our Amygdala intuitively believes everything will be fine if we can only get a banana – if we can just get back to that peak state of the **Big Win** she remembers when we felt fantastic, in control, invincible.

- But with no rational decision-making process awake and on duty telling us to call it a day, and an anxious, panicking **Amygdala** running the show, and a **Hypothalamus** pumping out **Dopamine** making us feel rewarded for taking the right action, we empty wallets, cards, bank accounts, get payday loans, and do all that as well until we are completely and utterly dry. We are no longer able to gamble.

- Within 30 minutes we feel like we have been mugged and cannot believe what we have done (again). These negative experiences are *not* logged in our underdeveloped and possibly defective **Insular** (which normally stores memories of bad experiences) and with each gambling session our mind's underlying neural circuitry becomes stronger and more resilient.

In order to break this cycle, we must set a new BALANCE point where our Neurotransmitters are being generated by natural methods at normal levels again, and our **Prefrontal Cortex** is stimulated in natural ways with Mindfulness and NAC techniques.

Less stress and anxiety will also place less strain on our **Amygdala**, causing it to start shrinking in size, and we begin to feel like we can cope again without having to escape.

#2 - Gambling is a CONNECTION Disorder

For whatever reason – perhaps an undeveloped brain, childhood trauma or some other adverse circumstances, we did not **mature** properly.

And when there was an interruption to our normal 'healthy' Connection, we instead used Gambling as **Substitute** Connection – a substitute for:

- Connection with a *significant other*
- Connection with our *mother* or our *family*
- Connection with our *social environment*
- Connection with *ourselves*

Connection is a reoccurring theme in this book. Going on the different studies like RatPark and Vietnam, it would appear that Addiction can be automatically repaired by finding or re-establishing the Connection that all humans need with others.

Without constant connection our brains don't develop and mature as they should, and we remain in an isolated state of distress that we feel compelled to self-medicate and escape from.

But when we're gambling we feel at home in our own skin, like we belong. We feel grateful, a deep **Connection**, a maternal bond, with whatever woke us up (a feeling that perhaps we did not experience enough of when we were little).

As the Six Human Needs tells us, we will meet the need for Love / Connection one way or the other, good or bad. If we can't get Love, we'll settle for Connection. Which is where our old friend *Dopamine* comes in.

- Are we trying to get the feeling of Connection from Dopamine?

- Have we really been trying to *simulate feelings of comfort & connection* by manipulating our neurotransmitters like Serotonin and Oxytocin? Has Gambling become our mistress that we spend more Time and Money on than anything else, in order to try and feel LOVE?

- Are we trying to connect and *bond* with a machine, a screen, or a fantasy world rather than the people closest to us? To find *"the warm hug of a mother"*?

- What of the connection with ourselves? We're so busy rushing, risking, stressing, distracting and escaping – are we really that uneasy with ourselves to be quiet for even a minute?

- Are we trying to fill the void left by our lack of *Growth* and *Contribution*, to take our tortured minds off the fact that we are stagnating and life is passing us by?

If we do not meet our need for Connection and the other human needs in healthy ways, we become out of BALANCE as a person which leads us down many wrong roads, creating yet more problems for ourselves.

So Which is it... a Brain or Connection Disorder?

Possibly both. But one thing's for certain:

- First we start off *participating* in gambling for entertainment or distraction

- Then we start *using* gambling as a substitute for something else, or a way to self-medicate our way through unresolved problems

- Then gambling uses <u>US</u> - leaving us empty & unfulfilled

In terms of how we break the cycle, BALANCE is the common factor to both. We can either approach it from a:

- **BRAIN** perspective - We try to balance our neurotransmitters and reprogram our limiting beliefs and neural circuitry (*which brings about a change in our resulting behaviour*) or

- **HUMAN NEEDS** perspective - We try to balance our Six Human Needs, especially Connection, in order to bring about a change in our behaviour (*which brings about a change in our underlying brain circuits*).

Personally I do BOTH as I not only want to prevent Addiction from wrecking my life and other peoples, but I also want to be happy and live to my full potential.

Trying to live a *multi-centred way of life* is a goal that helps with both approaches. But it's not easy and after 25 years I am still a work in progress!

The Only Way to Win is Not to Play

1993: When it was time for me to do something about my gambling problem, I remember telling someone that if I could just have £10 on a Saturday and be satisfied with that, I'd be a happy camper. Spoken like a true addict who can't even bear the thought of not getting his next fix (or rather a chimp that wants his banana).

And that was after 10 years of chaos, multiple rockbottoms, and a court case!

Once you have crossed the line, it would seem you can't go back. I've seen people attempt it, but never seen anyone return to gambling without ruining their life again. I've seen a lot of people try sample bets after a year or so, and very soon they are back into the same pattern and levels of damage (if not greater). A couple of people I knew even went 10 and 15 years each without a bet, then tried it again - didn't go well either.

So my own thoughts are once you've got a history of using something in an extreme way – of abusing it – then probably best to stay well clear of it! It's simply not worth risking the life that you've built up and everything that goes with in - your relationship, house, savings, etc. I personally never want to be that guy again so am staying well clear of it. I don't gamble with my recovery.

And at any time that I think that life is becoming too boring without Gambling, then frankly I need to do more work on myself, and on my life.

Your New Normal

A much better plan is tie up your Time and Money properly, and work the Five Daily Programmes. You'll be back on track in no time. There will be a lot to sort out, yes, but even a journey of a thousand miles starts with a single step. Do one step and then another – don't look up or look down, just put one foot in front of the other, and you'll soon learn to walk again.

Build momentum. Make a start with the Safeguards and give one of the Programmes maximum effort. Then add another Programme the following week and so on. Also add in the mental exercises detailed in this book as they will massively accelerate your progress.

- Stress can be a BIG trigger, so use the Daily Programme to manage potential stress and keep it as far away as humanly possible.

- Managing your time properly is critical, so give your Daily Programme TOP priority. Sticking to it and ticking things off as you go is your only focus.

- And use the exercise and diet tips to keep your neurotransmitters topped up naturally, reducing cravings and urges.

  Before you know it you will be back in balance, and your new 'normal' will be living a happy, rewarding, productive day – **ONE DAY AT A TIME.**

It may be sometime before you can use money normally again, but it will come in time if you keep things on track. And even when you and your Helper feel you can start handling very small amounts again, keep those safeguards in place for longer than you think necessary, just in case – there's no harm in it. If you want full access early on then your alarm bells should be going off.

But as I said at the beginning - Gambling is not the primary problem, *it's an attempt to solve a problem*. So the sooner you work out what that problem is, the sooner you can address it and move on.

In my experience within a week or two of not having a bet, the fog starts to lift and the mind starts to clear. At that point whatever emotion(s) you are trying to avoid or self-medicate yourself through – stress, anxiety, heartbreak, grief, boredom, childhood trauma, family drama, low self-esteem, lack of variety in your life, stale relationship, lack of connection, or something else – usually becomes apparent.

Then take a calm, mindful approach and start talking with whoever you think the conversation needs to be with.

<u>Draw a line under the past.</u>

Yesterday's gone
and nothing we can do will change that.

The money's gone too - you've already chased it
more than you should.

Tomorrow hasn't happened yet
and we'll deal with it when we get there.

Live today
and discover who you can be

One Day at a Time

* * *

What's Next?

Well, get on with it - IMMEDIATELY!

Get **Safeguards** in place to ensure you follow through this time.

Understand your **Triggers** & create alternative actions. Avoiding the urges is easier than having them.

Get some **Structure** into your life using the Daily Programmes - they will help enormously.

Pay attention to how you meet your **Six Human Needs**, and how you meet the needs of others.

Balance out your **Neurotransmitters** naturally with a Dopamine & Serotonin rich **Diet** to help with urges & withdrawal symptoms. Stay hydrated, and get some regular exercise in order to produce your own feel good neurotransmitters.

Practice **Mindfulness** throughout the day and start making conscious choices. Use it to manage your mind and release the old brain patterns as they fire, simply by halting your attention, observing what's going on in your mind & body, then making a better choice.

Anytime you feel afraid, unsure or at risk simply interrupt your pattern with the TRIAD technique and immediately **Change your State** by changing your Body, Focus or Language.

\# Practice reprogramming your mind with **NAC** techniques and overwrite those old beliefs and misfiring patterns. People use NAC to install better circuits, better behaviours, and give themselves an upgrade.

Focus on **TODAY** only, the present moment,
the **HERE AND NOW**,
one day at a time, one hour at a time.

I broke free of Gambling Addiction, and have had the privilege to know and help others who have done the same. When you no longer use the old destructive patterns they start to wither and die, and no longer have any power over you. The body's internal balance resets itself back to normal quicker than you think, and your finances too.

Remember, it's not about giving something up. It's about *gaining something in return* – a rewarding and balanced **multi-centred life** that you can enjoy and be proud of.

It's time to turn your *Shoulds* into *MUSTS*.

Stop existing, start LIVING and become the person you were meant to be.

THIS IS YOUR LIFE.

DO WHAT YOU LOVE, AND DO IT OFTEN.

IF YOU DON'T LIKE SOMETHING, CHANGE IT.
IF YOU DON'T LIKE YOUR JOB, QUIT.
IF YOU DON'T HAVE ENOUGH TIME, STOP WATCHING TV.
IF YOU ARE LOOKING FOR THE LOVE OF YOUR LIFE, STOP;
THEY WILL BE WAITING FOR YOU WHEN YOU
START DOING THINGS YOU LOVE.
STOP OVER ANALYZING, ALL EMOTIONS ARE BEAUTIFUL.
WHEN YOU EAT, APPRECIATE
LIFE IS SIMPLE. EVERY LAST BITE.
OPEN YOUR MIND, ARMS, AND HEART TO NEW THINGS
AND PEOPLE, WE ARE UNITED IN OUR DIFFERENCES.
ASK THE NEXT PERSON YOU SEE WHAT THEIR PASSION IS,
AND SHARE YOUR INSPIRING DREAM WITH THEM.
TRAVEL OFTEN; GETTING LOST WILL HELP FIND YOURSELF
SOME OPPORTUNITIES ONLY COME ONCE, SEIZE THEM.
LIFE IS ABOUT THE PEOPLE YOU MEET, AND
THE THINGS YOU CREATE WITH THEM
SO GO OUT AND START CREATING.
LIFE IS LIVE YOUR DREAM
AND SHARE
SHORT. YOUR PASSION.

Chapter 29
The Road Less Travelled

It's fair to say that I been on *"The Road Less Travelled"* and if you're reading this, so have you.

ACT I

After being thrown out of university for not even turning up to lectures, I landed a job in London in the music business. Richard Branson sent me an invite to join him for a party on his houseboat, but I was too busy gambling to attend. We had a number #1 act that I never even went to see – because I was gambling. Within 12 months of that I was sleeping rough. *Thank You Gambling, you chewed me up and spat me out.*

When I got back on my feet, girlfriends, friends, family – everything - came second to gambling. It consumed my life from 18 to 28. I don't actually remember most of my twenties.

My gambling journey has taken me to some terrifying places. Thousands of hours of gambling with nothing to show for it, different towns and different jobs but always the same outcome. Even down and out on the streets of

London, sleeping in doorways and begging in tube stations. I felt like I was insane, not all there.

But thankfully – and I am very proud of this – it was a two part drama and ACT II has been a *lot* better than ACT I.

ACT II

At 28 following a court appearance I decided to stand up to my problem. I vowed to do *whatever* it took to leave gambling in the past, and start living. To *never* live like that again. To never have to lie like that again. To never be that guy again. Something deep inside of me told me I was better than this.

I didn't have any skills or qualifications, and wanted to teach myself "computers". But I was broke, didn't have a PC, and even if I did was computer phobic and couldn't use Word or send an email (literally).

But I wanted a new life, so started from where I was, with what I'd got. I didn't have any money so learned from out of date books borrowed from the library (pre-google). I didn't have a desk so got a free one from a skip. It was so bent it was more like a wooden hammock than a desk. And I piled up PC magazines as a makeshift monitor stand. My girlfriend bought me an old PC on finance, and I managed to download a hooky copy of Microsoft Office over a dialup modem which tied the phone line up for 2 days solid. And when it finally finished downloading and installed, it was in Polish.

But I had made a start and kept at it. I didn't have any customers so offered to work for free, to get experience and build up a portfolio I could show others. Eventually I got one paying customer and earned £6,000 that year. It wasn't much, but because I wasn't gambling it felt like a lot of money. I bought some new books and read each five or six times each until they sort of made sense.

I got more clients through the first one and then started my own web design company. I didn't know what I was doing half the time, but learned on the job. A few years later I started another company. We created our own CRM software and over the next few years supplied it to companies in 17 countries around the world. I employed a team of people and partnered with Microsoft. And while that was going on, got married and had kids too.

Everything was going in the right direction until May 2017 when two things happened within the space of 2 weeks. My company was hacked and completely destroyed overnight, and I had a heart operation. Had a couple of minor strokes as well which killed off part of my brain (my friends say it's an improvement).

My own father had died of a heart attack around the same age. Lying there in the hospital bed, I thought about the fact that they had given me 2 years to live but had now fixed me up. And I had worked out how I could repair my brain myself. But it made me really think about who I was

- if that had been it, would I have been happy? No not really.

You see over the last 25 years as well as trying to do an impression of normal human being, I've been helping other problem gamblers get over their addiction. I setup GA groups, helplines, and organised prison meetings for the poor bastards that been locked up for gambling-related crimes.

And when I lay there thinking about what I wanted my third act to be, it wasn't software. What I was best at wasn't computers - it was people, specifically helping people like me. I understand problem gamblers and addicts in general because I've *been* one (and from time to time still do a good impression of one). I have done my best to help Gambling Addicts for over a quarter of century. Recovery IS my expertise - although that will come as a surprise to friends and business partners as it's not something I have discussed outside of the family before.

ACT III

So... I decided I was going to dedicate the next 10 years to making sure there are more resources for problem gamblers and their families (on next page).

Please do join me on social media and my recovery network, and be sure to share your story with me and how this book has helped you.

My projects rely on donations, and if you like what I'm doing to help then please donate at **CrowdfundMe.co.uk** – every little helps. And rate the book on Amazon please, it helps more people know about it. There are 2 people a day committing gambling-related suicide and we simply *have* to do more to save more young lives.

You can most likely find me on or around **GamHelp.org** - my new online community for problem gamblers and their families.

And finally, if I can break free then **SO CAN YOU!** The biggest obstacle I faced wasn't gambling, it was *myself*. It will be the same for you. You <u>have</u> to get out of your own way, get some structure into your day, reconnect with life and re-join the human race.

USE THE PROCESSES AND TECHNIQUES YOU HAVE LEARNED, STARTING RIGHT NOW.

You may have read this book, but if you're anything like me you haven't actually *read* it, you've just flicked through it.. Now go back and **<u>READ</u>** the thing properly, and make notes in the margin. Read, Read again, and DO.

If you're not feeling emotional after the exercises, then you need to repeat and open up more. Repeat, repeat and repeat until you *feel it* in your heart. Give yourself the leverage that you need to change.

Yes <u>DO</u> the exercises. This isn't a dress rehearsal, this is real life – stop sleepwalking through it and WAKE UP!

**Remember, it's not how you start
but how you finish that counts.**

What's *your* next ACT going to be like?

* * *

About the Author

Mike Chatha (pronounced *Char-ta*) was lining up at the seaside arcades from at the age of 8 onwards and was hopelessly addicted to gambling from 18-28, during which period he caused himself and the people around him a lot of problems.

He paid for his gambling with lost relationships, lost education, business ventures that never got started, lost homes, lost health, lost family, lost friends, lost sanity and lost money. It landed him in court at the age of 28 watching his worried mother say nice things to a jury about him. His father couldn't be there as the stress of Mike's actions had already contributed to his fatal heart attack at just 56.

But for the last 25 years has been a different story. Mike taught himself IT, web design and software development, and then founded and ran his own international CRM company. As well as getting his own life back on track, Mike has been actively helping others overcome their gambling problems, and helping their families come to terms with what has been going on.

Early on he worked out that the people that helped others were the ones that managed to stay off gambling themselves. So he helped start several Gamblers Anonymous (GA) groups, performed Prison visits, setup and manned Helplines, did various television programmes, helped run GA as an organisation, and basically tried to help out however he could.

Mike now works exclusively helping Problem Gamblers through his not-for-profit company, Back on Track Project CIC.

Passionate about helping those affected by Gambling Addiction, Mike is currently working on a number of help resources:

GamblingAddiction.blog   Mike's own personal gambling blog (where you will find further info about some of the content in the book and other things)

GamHelp.org   Online community for problem gamblers and their families. If you found this book helpful then please drop by and say hello. Better still share your story on there in the Stories section and help others just by being there – worked for me!

Gamware.co.uk   Software company that will be releasing a range of tools and apps to help problem gamblers. Currently trying to raise money at CrowdFundMe.co.uk

GamblingIndustry.co.uk   Website which highlights Gambling Harm and Operators that take advantage of vulnerable addicts

You can also follow him on Twitter **@GamblerHelp**

Everything Mike does is privately funded without the help of industry or anyone else. He relies on donations at: **CrowdfundMe.co.uk** and would greatly appreciate your support.

The more you help, the more he can do to help the gambler that still suffers.

* * *

APPENDICES

Appendix I
Guidance for Partners, Friends & Families

Is [x] a Compulsive Gambler?

A friend, partner of family member might consider:

1. Do they look physically worse than they used to?
2. Do they make excuses on a regular basis?
3. Do they run out of money or borrow money regularly?
4. Are there multiple unexplained withdrawals on a bank statement?
5. Do they have unexplained absences from home?
6. Do you think they are frequently lying about their whereabouts?
7. Do they tell different stories to various family members and friends?
8. Have they become more insular, spending more & more time alone?
9. Do they become evasive or argumentative when asked about their activities?
10. Do they seem protective over their computer, tablet or mobile phone?
11. Do they seem protective over the post or home telephone?
12. Are they less reliable than they used to be?
13. Are they less loving or affectionate than they used to be?

14. Do they go to bed after you or get up earlier for no good reason?
15. Do they having difficulty sleeping?
16. Are they more irritable and have rapid or dramatic mood swings?
17. Have they lost interest in hobbies/activities that they once found rewarding?
18. Do they spend time with friends who you think may have a gambling problem?
19. Is only the minimum amount being paid on bills?
20. Has money gone missing from your wallet or purse, bank account or a child's piggy bank?

How did they score?

- 1-5 Points
  A person without a gambling addiction will typically score 4 or less, but there are still signs
  of a problem beginning that should be addressed before it gets out of hand.

- 6+ Points
  A person with a compulsion or full-blown addiction will have a YES to **at least 6** of the questions.

- **7-14 Points**
  A person is who is no longer in control or their activity will have a YES for between 7-14 questions, and specifically YES to number [2], [8] and [16].

  [2]: *Do they make regular excuses?*
  [8]: *Are they more insular, spending more time alone?*
  [16]: *Have they lost interest in activities or hobbies?*

If the score is reasonably high (ie. over 6) then there is clearly a problem which is most probably gambling. There may have already been material damage.

But someone having an affair or with a sex problem will also score highly on this test, and may not have been gambling at all.

So do nothing for now until you have read the rest of this information.

How to Spot a Gambling Addict

It's difficult to spot an addict as very few actually admit to being one, even with a gun to their head! But if you know what you are looking for, there ARE addiction signs.

Gambling Addicts are either in Recovery or Denial, there is no halfway house.

When confronted the Addict will usually do everything possible to deny it.

The Signs

Most major addictions often display subtle signs of addiction:

- A functioning **alcoholic** drinking might lose weight and become late & forgetful, which they attempt to conceal through excuses and stories
- A person with an **eating disorder** might gain or lose 5kg a month, which they try to conceal with excuses and baggy clothes
- A **drug addict** may have a permanent cold or marks on his body, which they try to conceal & explain in various ways
- A **Gambler** who has lost their entire month's wages might come up with some detailed excuses how he didn't get paid properly, or didn't get his bonus

A gambling addict is difficult to spot... but not impossible.

They are hidden in plain sight, but like a magician they use misdirection and other methods to dupe those right in front of them.

To them it's nothing personal – they *have to* lie in order to keep their awful secret safe, and at some level they will have convinced themselves that they are doing you a favour by keeping this from you.

But once you know what you've looking for, a gambling Addict is in fact remarkably easy to spot. So much so that you will feel incredibly stupid for not having seen it a long time ago.

Typical Excuses/Explanations

Have a look at the list below. Every normal person or Gambler will give the odd excuse.

But a **Gambling Addict** will cycle through <u>ALL</u> of these on a regular basis, maintaining the lie by remembering what they have & haven't told you over the last 6 months.

Listen out for the following addiction signs:

Money

- *They paid me late..*
- *I didn't get my bonus this month..*
- *They got my pay wrong..*
- *I lent my money to someone else..*
- *The bank have made a mistake, I'll sort it..*
- *Someone has used my card, call fraud protection..*
- *I was mugged, honestly..*

Time

- *Sorry I didn't realise the time..*
- *Can't believe I lost my watch..*
- *I broke/lost my phone..*
- *Traffic's bad, I'll be home late..*
- *They want me to work late again..*

Location

- *I've been at work doing a 12 hour day!*
- *Of course I didn't go into the bookies, how could I?*

- *Someone had the idea to go [somewhere / to a friends/ for a drink] and I just went along..*
- *I told you I would be out – you just don't remember?*

Communications

- *Sorry, I didn't realise you were trying to get hold of me..*
- *Service was poor, no reception..*
- *Something must be wrong with my phone..*
- *Sorry I ran out of phone credit..*
- *My phone just died..*

How Did I Not Notice?

Before you start beating yourself up, remember that your blind spot has born out of trust, and fully monopolised and *conditioned* by the Gambler.

Note that your Gambler would have felt progressively worse about this, but it was the only way they could continue to feed their addiction – without you knowing.

So if you are still trying to work out if your other half is a gambling addict, start by picking up their phone or go through their pockets/bank statements and see how nervous/agitated they get.

If they do, look them in the eye and asked them if there is something they want to tell you?

Do not speak again until they speak first and either tell you (maybe true, maybe another lie) or they get aggressive and leave – the hallmark of an addict backed into a corner.

But even though a Gambler's heart can be beating like an Olympic sprinter, their face will remain completely calm – a deception skill they have learned to master over time.

Why Don't They Just Come Clean?

Seriously? The gambler will do anything and everything to keep his shameful secret from being discovered by the people around them. All the lies they have told, and lies to cover up the lies.

And then there's the money. All that money that should have been spent on other things for other people.

And then there's the debts that you do not know about yet – the credit cards, accounts, overdrafts and loans.

The Awful Truth

If the family or loved one was to hear the truth about the THOUSANDS of hours spent gambling when they been told for many months/years that this person had been doing something else entirely, they would feel deceived, abused and betrayed by the gambler and be out of there in a heartbeat! At least that's what the Gambler believes.

And if the partner was also to learn about the substantial amount of money spent on gambling when instead they had previously been told again & again that were short of money or excuses about not receiving that pay rise or bonus, then again they would feel robbed and violated.

So in the gambler's scrambled mind there is <u>NEVER</u> a good time to disclose this information voluntarily. This explains why 9 out of 10 gamblers have to be caught out, rather than confessing first. Incidentally the 1 of out 10 that *does* confess is rarely confessing the whole truth, just their version of it.

Do They Ever Confess on their Own?

Things need to reach a point of no return, where either:

- The gambler gets found out (having raising suspicion by staying out longer, not coming home, having no money, being seen in the betting shop, getting letters or visits from finance companies, etc)
- The partner challenges the gambler with their suspicions and gives them an ultimatum

When this moment happens, it is simultaneously the BEST and the WORST moment of the gambler's life. They are consumed with shame over their actions, but feel the huge burden lifting that they have carried alone for so long.

More often than not there will have been elements of Manipulation, Misdirection or an absence of the whole truth within this confession. They will attempt to **limit the damage** and **lessen the impact** of their terrible revelations. Even then they will attempt to manage the situation, as it has become an ingrained habit.

If a gambler does confess he may want to run back to the pub, casino, or their laptop. Here they can self-medicate their frustrations & fears, and somehow convince themselves that they have the situation under control.

Gambling is the only addiction where *One More* is seen as the solution.

Credit Check

One of the first things you should be doing is to credit check yourself using one of the many online services.

For those in the UK I often recommend a free 30-day trial on a service called CheckMyFile.com which searches all the major credit agencies in a single search, as well as the people sharing the same address.

This will tell you if your name has been used without your consent to support any finance application. Over the years I have met spouses who had no idea that they had a second mortgage or a large secured loan on their property – not nice to find out. So get the facts immediately to remove any doubt.

The search should also show if your credit score has been affected by anyone living with you. So if you have a partner in the house and they have defaulted in loans that you don't yet know about, this will show up.

And while we're on it, double check all your bank statements for anything strange.

Confronting a Gambler

If challenged about their activities, the gambler has a number of tried & tested strategies to get out of the spotlight:

- **Manipulation** – turn the questions back onto the questioner by making their absence somehow the fault of the other person

- **Misdirection** – in their explanations reference people that are not present

- **More Lies** – introducing some new (false) information, creating a multi-layered lie or further fabrication of the truth

Therefore you should not attempt to confront a person over their gambling until you have more facts at your disposal, ideally some concrete proof from betting slips, account withdrawals, card transactions, internet history, or other proof.

Debt and Money Management

Problem gambling creates debt. In the UK the gambling Industry takes £38 million pounds a Day (£14Billion a year). They make money, you don't - you OWE money.

There's an old saying: *When you are in hole, stop digging!* So as of now you are going to be HONEST and TRANSPARENT about what you owe and to whom.

- COME CLEAN – Tell your family/other half about your debts – ALL of them – so that they can help you pay these people back. There may be a debt that you feel you can't tell them yet. But you *have* to tell them now or it will be much worse later.

- WRITE TO THE DEBTORS – Write (not call) and inform them you have a Mental Health issue (specifically a compulsive gambling problem) that you are currently addressing, and ask them for a current statement. Also ask them to freeze the interest. Even though you may have defaulted on these loans, you still have rights. And the loan company still must handle you correctly in accordance with the laws protecting the vulnerable.

- BEGIN PAYING OFF THE DEBTS – Obviously the debts need prioritising and it's important that you pay the debts over the *longest* term possible, as it's a lasting reminder of the consequences of your actions. Ask debtors to freeze the interest, and go for 5 or 10 year repayment terms. But repay you will, and it will help fend off your next bet. By all means prioritise the high interest credit cards etc to get paid first, no point in wasting money. Make offers to pay back a bit a month – even £10 – no more sticking your head in the sand. Paying a bit a month will usually prevent or slow down any pending action.

If this section made you particularly anxious and sweaty, that's normal.

But remember that while you may owe an alarming amount of money, it is only that: Money. It's NOT as important as your Mental Health, and you <u>can</u> offer to pay a lot of it back slowly over time. Debtors might even write some of the debt off – but you must communicate with them and tell them about your gambling problem.

Bailouts

While the partner / family may offer to bail you out, you should politely NOT accept. This is *your* mess and YOU have to clean it up, no matter how slowly or how long it takes.

If you want any chance of overcoming your Gambling Addiction, you absolutely MUST take responsibility for your actions, no matter how painful that it. In my experience people that pay their debts – no matter how slowly – are x100 more likely to overcome their addiction and go on to establish a happy, productive life.

But if there is for any reason a bailout from family, then it must be paid back each month, no matter how small the amount to start with.

Debt Management Companies

If you have several debts it is advisable to talk a Debt Management company. Don't be embarrassed or ashamed, you will not be the first Problem Gambler they have seen, believe me! The advantage of going through such a company is that they have done this before.

You tell them everything, and they communicate with all your debtors and make arrangements to pay on your behalf. Where possible they can also negotiate the amount down, and have some of the debt written off. They will also advise you about the pros & cons of entering into an IVA (Individual Voluntary Arrangement) or Bankruptcy.

Before engaging such a company, a good place to start is the Citizens Advice Bureau:

https://www.citizensadvice.org.uk/debt-and-money/debt-solutions/individual-voluntary-arrangements

Appendix III
Deviations on the Road to Recovery

From the original transcript of a workshop given at the first International GA convention in the UK London, June 1985. Originally led by Iain Brown, MBE, Psychologist & Senior Lecturer at Glasgow University, Chairman of the European Society for the Study of Gambling. Edited, Updated and Expanded by Mike Chatha February 2019

#1 - Unbalanced Human Needs

Many recovering gamblers struggle to transition to a happy, productive life as they are still meeting some of their first four Human Needs in the wrong way, or not even attempting the last two!

Needs of:

The Personality: *Certainty, Variety, Significance, Love / Connection*

The Soul: *Growth, Contribution*

If the first four are all being met in productive ways and the last two are at least being attempted, the Gambler will enjoy a happy and lasting recovery and have no need of gambling.

#2 – Complacency

Thinking that you are cured or no longer doing what has been working for you is the fastest possible way back to gambling. Nearly every Gambler goes this phase a few weeks or a few months after quitting. Many try to handle money again like they are normal without any limits to access or accountability measures in place, while other try a few small bets. This is complacency: thinking that in this short time that you are better. Don't make this mistake – don't change a thing until at least 12 months. And even then, exercise caution – I have known many people go back to gambling after a year off, and it's even worse than before. So stay safe, it's your top priority.

#3 - Workaholism

For gamblers this is a subtly attractive cross-addiction or a deviation along the road to recovery. Workaholism is a righteous kind of addiction. In working to excess, gamblers are seen to restore the family fortunes and make amends. So other people tend to accept it and approve of it, even the wives and families of the workaholics themselves.

But when working becomes addictive too, it maintains the worker's isolation and distance from family and loved ones. Whereas before he avoided relating meaningfully to them by gambling, now he easily manages to do the same thing with a lot less hassle and some people even commend him for it! He can avoid social occasions and go on hiding his lack of social skills and escape just as before, and he still has another single monoculture focus of his life which helps simplify decisions and leaves him safely cocooned in a narrow restricted little life space, confined to his impregnable fortress of virtue and such a feeling of misery that he feels he has more than earned the RIGHT to have a little flutter again.

#4 – Alcoholism

Increased drinking when a person stops gambling is an obvious cross-addiction. Sometimes the transition from gambling to alcohol happens dramatically within a fortnight. More common than a straight swap of one addiction for another, are some classic interactions between drinking and gambling. Common occurrences are first, where drinking is used as the gateway to gambling, and, second, where one is used as a decoy to draw the enemy's attention away from the other.

Where drinking is used as a **gateway to gambling**, drink in itself is not much of a problem as gambling only takes place following drinking. As the two are partners in crime, the drinking has to go. In this instance total abstinence from drinking is as necessary as abstinence from gambling. True, the gambler does not have a drinking problem, is not an alcoholic, but she does have a drink related problem. She needs to do something about her drinking just as much as any true alcoholic.

The second most common interaction between drinking and gambling is where drinking is used as a **decoy** for gambling or vice versa. Here the gambler goes for help about his drinking and all the attention of everyone is devoted to his drinking - which allows him to go on gambling heavily unnoticed (which is his real problem).

Of course alcoholism has some of the same effects as gambling. The simple cycle of immediate pleasure at the expense of long-term misery is restored when a gambler turns to drinking. The new drinker can still manage to live something like his old narrow life and so avoids facing other problems such his lack of social skills. Above all he can maintain his isolation, avoid getting too close to his family, just as before.

#5 - Drugs (Legal and Illegal)

Our experience is that gamblers do not seem to use a lot of illegal drugs. Cannabis is too mild to be interesting to them. The falling price of Cocaine and its ability to instantly awaken the Prefrontal Cortex is to be noted. I have known a few gamblers dabble in both. Sometimes dealing in drugs is a source of gambling money and then there can be a cross addiction between gambling and stimulant drugs.

#6 – Porn

Porn provides another way for the Compulsive Gambler to escape him or herself. Once the gambling is under control and the finances are starting to stablise, it is all too easy for the gambler to stay up late or go the bathroom, fire up a device, and escape themselves again and again. Porn is a ready source of Dopamine, and a lot cheaper than gambling. But if the Gambler goes down this road, he is still failing to rebuild the Connections with the important people in his life – in fact he is actively avoiding it. He is still in isolation which is feeding the old demons. Partner relationships cannot repair or flourish while one of the parties is having an affair with a screen.

#7 - Smoking

Smoking is recognised as the most difficult addiction to get rid of. The problem is that the pleasure of inhalation is instant (nicotine hits the brain within about half a minute of intake into the lungs) and it is repeated so often that the habit becomes unusually strong. Also, in contrast to compulsive gambling and alcoholism, the pay off in pain, misery and ill health is remote and far away in the future. Smokers who give up, have the highest relapse rate (next to eating addictions) and the greatest long term failure rate. Sound advice would be if you still haven't yet got over your gambling addiction, don't try to give up smoking at the same time. It could prove very demoralising for you. But later when your gambling recovery has stabilised and you have not gambled for, say, one to two years, you should try and will quite possibly succeed. [Author: I personally quit 12 months after gambling.]

#8 - Caffeine (Tea, Coffee, Caffeine drinks)

Both of these are fairly quick acting stimulant drugs. They give you an immediate lift which is why we use them to wake up our Prefrontal Cortex. Neither are at all serious addictions except for a small minority of people, but, if carried to excess, they can have some important effects that most people do not know about. Like all addictions they provide a form of short-term pleasure, almost pampering, a way of saying to the child inside yourself - see I love you after all, even if nobody else does. An American psychologist has described this as Giving yourself a stroke. We all need strokes of this kind from time to time.

More seriously, if you take more than seven large cups of average strength in a day, you begin to run risks of broken sleep patterns, restlessness and anxiety. The trouble is that, just like with any other addiction, too much caffeine makes you feel so bad with lack of sleep and nerviness that you think you need some more, and so on and so on. Clinical Psychologists have been discovering that some cases of chronic anxiety are really only mostly the effect of caffeinism. Whenever the coffee drinking habit is broken the anxiety goes down to acceptable levels.

#9 - Unfaithfulness

All major addictions disrupt sexual relations. Many addictions disrupt sexual performance for purely psychological reasons. It usually happens in two stages.

Addiction weakens the relationship. Mistrust, anger, anxiety, indifference and neglect become the major currency of feelings and actions between the two partners. Often these negative feelings persist unresolved for months or even years, and they make it more difficult, if not impossible, to win through to the positive joys which can go with sexual relations. It only takes one partner to feel the difficulties and the other usually becomes affected too.

Most people, when they first come for help with a major addiction, have problems in their relationship of this kind. Most relationships rebalance themselves naturally after it is clear that the addiction is under control. But it is a great mistake to try to rush into the full restoration of broken sexual relations after only a short period free of gambling just because you feel so much better. Time is needed on both sides to restore the atmosphere of trust and security which is the essential background for really joyful sexual relations.

Broken or patchy relationships may make for damaged self-esteem and make one or both partners more vulnerable to the attractions of others. Even people who normally would avoid it carefully, often find themselves looking for reassurance and appreciation, or wanting to take revenge. They get into unfaithfulness to major and minor degrees for a host of emotional reasons. Some get into unfaithfulness just when they are happiest, even happiest with their partner, almost just by way of celebration.

An affair has obvious addictive qualities too. It lifts the spirits, fills the mental horizons, dominates the feelings and determines moods, produces a new dream world and provides a temporary means of escape. But, above all it is short term pleasure replacing long term misery. Undoubtedly, for some, affairs become addictive and one follows another as soon as possible because the period in between is so awful.

#10 - Eating

Some of us turn to food as the great consolation. This is an addictive problem to which total abstinence is NOT an answer! Some food addicts even try that, with fasting and feasting. More common is controlled eating with a whole world of expensive diets and conflicting advice. Gamblers are not very prone to food addictions but if they are, and you seem to have tried everything, remember that unsuccessful attempts to diet actually cause you to eat more in the long run. Try the alternative cure which may well be the real solution - more exercise. Don't focus on weight loss, focus instead on body composition and how your clothes fit. Exercise has been shown to frequently cut down your appetite, make you want to smoke and drink less and improves your sleep pattern - all simultaneously. Exercise also helps generate all the same neurotransmitters that Gambling used to do, but in a natural healthy way.

#11 - Living Beyond Your Means

Gamblers and money don't go together, even in recovery. Spending is well known as a short-term pleasure which can lead to long term misery and heavy spenders have many of the same addictive patterns of thinking, feeling and behaving as other addicts. Spending can mean so many things to the spender but, above all means status. Big spender equals high roller. But there are other meanings too. Spending on others makes amends, satisfies feelings of guilt. Spending on oneself may be like an assurance of love to a loveless child. It helps keep the feelings of expansive omnipotence and power that used to go with some stages of gambling. While the spree is on, it successfully helps avoid the more complex problems of real life but eventually, of course, like the gambler who always loses, so too, the bills always come home.

#12 - Dishonesty

For many, especially for gamblers but for some drinkers and unfaithful people too, lying becomes a natural way of life. It's easier to tell someone what they want to hear, than tell them the truth which will lead to questions. We avoid questions as we're told so many lies we struggle to keep track of them. Lying is an escape. It avoids reality and protects oneself and others from the truth. Some can lie so convincingly to themselves as well as to others that they lose sight of the truth altogether and end up in some bizarre play-act of a life or in a state of hopeless confusion. Others work so hard at maintaining a complex web of lies to all, that they exhaust themselves before they have begun the real business of life. Lying can easily be seen as another instance of short-term gain for long term loss. If someone is not gambling but still lying, you can expect them to be back gambling shortly.

Middle-Term Toleration for Transition Addictions

A *transition addiction* offers the possibility of change, of movement to some other state, to some place in life where there is no addiction and less possibility of any other addictions. So when coming off Gambling and you're spending a lot of time working and down the gym, this can work well to start with but needs to become more *multi-centered* over time.

Long Term Diversification

True recovery for many people will mean that their lives, instead of being centered around one single activity - a monoculture - become diversified into several different major activities of nearly equal importance. Partner, Children, Family, Friends, Work, Sport, Recreation, Learning and Community are just some. **A Multi-Centered way of Life**, vastly different from our old tunnel vision life.

The aim must be to concentrate on the areas of life

that, as an addict, they used to neglect. The ordinary non-addicted person tends to have several (at least two or three) different areas of importance or focus of concern in his life, (eg. his work, his family, his friends) no one of which totally dominates and overrules all the rest.

As the recovering gambler puts more time and effort into each of these areas, it begins to pay off, and work, family etc become rewarding again. At first the effort and pain are often very great, but a little success breeds more success. Sometimes the unlearning of an addictive way of life that has taken years to establish and the learning of a new multicentered life can be a long, difficult and painful process and each addict is to some extent alone because each new life is unique.

Until the diversification of interests, activities and concerns takes place, the Gambler will still remain a little more at risk of a cross addiction or a deviation along the road to recovery than they need be and their recovery will be less complete than it could be.

Even after a reasonable degree of diversification has been achieved, the maintenance of a non-addictive way of life can never be an easy or careless responsibility. It's easy to slip back into tunnel vision, so always be aware of the balance in how you spend your time.

Letting Go the Learned Pattern of Rewards in the Old Addictive Way of Life

After a year or two without gambling the diversification into a multi-centered way of life has not taken place, it could be for one of two reasons:

- Not enough intelligent effort has been put into attempting the new multicentered way of life, or
- That more help is needed to get it in place.

It is likely that one or more of the hidden advantages of the old addictive ways of life is standing in the way. So, means have to be found of identifying the block and giving it up too. Perhaps the question should be asked:

What is it about the addictive way of life that I still want to cling to?

What is it that I most want to avoid? Intimacy? The full range of my feelings? Social life? Meaninglessness? Giving up the moral high ground as a partner?

Dialogue, Listening, Learning, Acceptance, and a willingness to leave the past behind are the keys to moving forward.

Use the tools available – **The Six Humans Needs** (yours and other peoples) and the **Daily Programme** to kickstart your multi-centered life. It may fell weird to start but soon it will feel entirely normal.

Appendix IV
Odds & Ends
An Insight into Probability

Simply speaking, *odds* is the term used to describe the chances a person placing a bet has of winning.

In gambling:

- Odds are the chances of winning
- Odds are always against the person placing the bet
- The house always has the edge

In every betting game, the odds are against the player. That means that the house (the casino, bingo hall, racetrack, lottery commission etc.) is absolutely *guaranteed*, mathematically, to win over time.

For every millionaire that is created from lottery winnings, there are millions of others who have lost their money!

The longer you gamble, the more likely it is you will lose.

Many people who develop problems associated with their gambling have the false belief that they will be able to 'beat the system', while others may not understand that the odds are against them and that over time they will lose money.

Comparing the Odds

The odds of winning the Lottery 6/49 are approximately 1 in 14 million.

- A person has a 1 in 3 million chance of sighting an UFO. That's almost x5 times more likely than winning the jackpot.

- You are more likely to die of a flesh-eating disease (1 in 1 million) than winning the lottery. That's x14 times more likely than winning the jackpot.

- You are more likely to be killed by lightening (1 in 56,439) than win the lottery. That's almost x250 times more likely than winning the jackpot.

- You are more likely to be killed in a traffic accident driving 16 km to purchase a ticket than winning the jackpot.

- Imagine you are standing blindfolded on a football field holding a pin. A friend has released an ant on the field. Your chance of piercing that ant with your pin is about one in 14 million, the same odds of winning the Lotto 6/49 jackpot.

- The odds of winning the top prize at maximum coin play on the slot machines ranges from 1 in 4,096 to 1 in 33,554,000.

Another way to look at the odds of winning the lottery jackpot:

Mrs. Jane Doe lives somewhere in Ontario.
Try reaching her by randomly dialling one of 12.5 million Ontario phone numbers.

Your odds of calling Mrs. Doe on the *first try* are better than winning the lottery.

Taken from
https://www.problemgambling.ca/gambling-help/gambling-information/what-are-odds.aspx

Appendix V
Return-To-Player (RTP)

Gaming machines, also called fruit machines, slots, Pokies or FOBTs, are required to clearly display the percentage return-to-player figure (% RTP), or the odds of winning a prize.

Gaming machines offer different prize amounts depending on their category.

It is important to realise however, that the % RTP is an average achieved over a significant number of game plays and NOT each time the gaming machine is played.

Average % RTP is generally measured over 10,000 or 100,000 games or greater for compensated and random machines respectively, dependent upon their category.

For example, if a gaming machine displays an 85% RTP, you should NOT expect to win an average of 85 pence for every £1 you stake during a playing session.

There is no statutory minimum percentage payout for a gaming machine.

RTP is best summed up by the UK Gambling Commission who published several pieces of guidance on their website.

ככ כ

Here are the key extracts:

*"It is important to realise however, that the **% RTP is an average achieved over a significant number of game plays and not each time the gaming machine is played.**

Average % RTP is generally measured over 10,000 or 100,000 games or greater for compensated and random machines respectively, dependent upon their category.

*For example, if a gaming machine displays an 85% RTP, you should **not** expect to win an average of 85 pence for every £1 you stake during a playing session.*

There is no statutory minimum percentage payout for a gaming machine."

At the time of writing the Gambling Commission seems to be aware that it would be relatively easy for a Gambling Operator to intentionally adjust the actual RTP away from its published RTP, in order to keep more of the money.

It has therefore felt it necessary to issue the following guidance:

*"Even though games must be tested prior to release (and after updates which may affect fairness) it is possible for a design, implementation or operational issue to **evade identification** during testing or deployment. This may affect the game's RTP and result in either an overpaying or underpaying product. "*

The same article goes on to state that Operators should not wait for **MILLIONS** of game plays which may take **YEARS** in order to calculate the average (!) and instead recommends 90 day sample periods.

Being Clear to Players

Gaming machines must make information available about their category, % RTP and whether they are compensated or random.

Compensated Machines

Compensated machines vary the chance of winning a prize as a result of the outcome from previous play. Where such a machine is below its target %RTP it may become more generous dependent upon design and vice versa, though the prize distribution is still determined by chance.

Random Machines

Random machines rely purely on statistical probabilities to achieve their target percentage return to player. The odds of achieving a win remain constant, and are not affected by previous wins or losses.

[taken from https://www.gamblingcommission.gov.uk/for-the-public/Safer-gambling/Consumer-guides/Machines-Fruit-machines-FOBTs/Gaming-machine-payouts-RTP.aspx]

Live RTP performance monitoring of games of chance

As of 1 September 2016 remote operators are required to monitor the performance of the games they offer. The core focus of this monitoring is to ensure random number generator (RNG) driven products are fair and achieving the designed return to player (RTP).

> *"Even though games must be tested prior to release (and after updates which may affect fairness) it is possible for a design, implementation or operational issue to evade identification during testing or deployment. This may affect the game's RTP and result in either an overpaying or underpaying product."*

[taken from https://www.gamblingcommission.gov.uk/for-gambling-businesses/Compliance/Sector-specific-compliance/Remote-and-software/Live-RTP-performance-monitoring.aspx]

The same article goes on to state that Operators should not wait for **millions** of game plays in order to calculate the average; and instead recommends 90 days sample times. But these are recommendations only, and the Gambling Operators are still free to configure the machines to payout however they see fit.

But for you, the recovering gambling Addict, the general takeaway is:

(1) Electronic gambling machines and Online Simulated Machines are simply running programs, and the Operator always wins (by design). The game is programmed so that THEY win, YOU lose.

(2) Each time you play you might think you have a good chance of winning, but in reality you don't.

(3) Even if you *could* somehow make yourself stop earlier you would still be losing - because the house always wins. But as you chase your losses with more money and can't walk away with your winnings, you're screwed.

Appendix VI
The Prefrontal Cortex
Further Reading

[This is just a small selection of articles and tests regarding PFC interference or shutdown. A search of Google Scholar and other resources suggest there could be in the region of 100+ studies with similar findings, dating back to the mid-nineties. It would appear that the academics have been aware of this for some time.]]

See **GamblingAddiction.blog** for copy of links.

Prefrontal cortex activity is reduced in gambling and nongambling substance users during decision-making - US National Library of Medicine – **2007** https://www.ncbi.nlm.nih.gov/pubmed/17274020

Pathological Choice: The Neuroscience of Gambling and Gambling Addiction - US National Library of Medicine – **2013** - https://www.ncbi.nlm.nih.gov/pmc/articles/PMC3858640/
Prefrontal Cortex Activity Reduced in Gambling & Nongambling Substance Users During Decision-Making – **2007** - http://psych.colorado.edu/~cuchangelab/publications/hutchison/2007/prefrontalcortexgambling.pdf

Gambling Addiction and the Brain – Brain Facts - **2015** https://www.brainfacts.org/Diseases-and-Disorders/Addiction/2015/Gambling-Addiction-and-the-Brain

Brain Cells in the Avian 'Prefrontal Cortex' Code for Features of Slot-Machine-Like Gambling – **2011** - https://journals.plos.org/plosone/article?id=10.1371/journal.pone.0014589

A neurocognitive comparison of cognitive flexibility and response inhibition in gamblers with varying degrees – **2011** -

https://www.cambridge.org/core/journals/psychological-medicine/article/neurocognitive-comparison-of-cognitive-flexibility-and-response-inhibition-in-gamblers-with-varying-degrees-of-clinical-severity/484DFBF908109D93CC3D9B08923AAB06

Impulsivity and response inhibition in alcohol dependence and problem gambling - **2009**
https://link.springer.com/article/10.1007/s00213-009-1645-x

Dysfunction of the prefrontal cortex in addiction: neuroimaging findings and clinical implications - US National Library – **2011** -
https://www.ncbi.nlm.nih.gov/pmc/articles/PMC3462342/

Role of Dopamine, the Frontal Cortex and Memory Circuits in Drug Addiction: Insight from Imaging Studies – **2002** -
https://www.sciencedirect.com/science/article/pii/S1074742702940992

Addiction and the Prefrontal Cortex An Interview with Rita Z. Goldstein, Ph.D. - **2007**
http://www.dana.org/Publications/ReportDetails.aspx?id=44208

Highway to addiction: how drugs and alcohol can hijack your brain – University of Cambridge – **2016** -
https://www.cam.ac.uk/research/features/highway-to-addiction-how-drugs-and-alcohol-can-hijack-your-brain

Neural circuits responsible for conscious self-control are highly vulnerable to even mild stress. When they shut down, primal impulses go unchecked and mental paralysis sets in - Library of Medicine – **2012**
https://www.ncbi.nlm.nih.gov/pmc/articles/PMC4774859/

Rats consume 3 times as much cocaine when the Amygdala is activated – **2017** - http://www.jneurosci.org/content/37/35/8330

Reduced insular size in Attention Deficit Hyperactivity Disorder – **2012** -
https://www.sciencedirect.com/science/article/pii/S0925492712002466

Different Contributions of the Human Amygdala and Ventromedial Prefrontal Cortex to Decision-Making – **1999** - http://www.jneurosci.org/content/19/13/5473

Characterization of the decision-making deficit of patients with ventromedial prefrontal cortex lesions – **2000** - https://academic.oup.com/brain/article/123/11/2189/255844

Frontal lobe dysfunction in pathological gambling patients – **2002** - https://www.sciencedirect.com/science/article/pii/S0006322301012276

Appendix VII
Stop When The Fun Stops..?

Much of the information in Appendix VI about a Gambler's prefrontal cortex shutting down has been in the public domain for 10-20 years and is readily available with the simplest of internet searches.

So it seems highly questionable that the main safety message presented by Industry to problem gamblers in 2019 is to ask that they voluntarily decide to 'stop when it's no longer fun' (as depicted in a common slogan below).

WHEN THE **FUN** STOPS **STOP**™

[copyright originator]

However the evidence suggests that someone with a gambling problem would *not be able to stop* because during the gambling activity a key part of their brain had failed to work normally, presumably as a direct result of exposure to the Gambling stimulus at the time, making them *incapable of making the decision to stop.*

Specifically, if someone has a gambling problem and were engaged in a gambling session, it could be potentially IMPOSSIBLE for them to stop due to their Prefrontal

Cortex being inhibited or shutting down as a *direct result* of the activity they are currently engaged in.

At least that's what the evidence of multiple experts and a volume of unrelated studies indicate. Incidentally the *type* of gambling (online, FOBT, casino, on premise, etc) and the type of game played (screen game, fruit machine, roulette, cards, etc) appears to be irrelevant.

If this is correct, then some hard questions need to be asked about why a £14Billion gambling industry with almost limitless resources didn't already know this? Or if they were aware, why haven't they already taken appropriate action?

[**NOTE:** While I am assuming the PFC shutdown applies to Problem Gamblers only, it presumably must happen to *EVERY* normal gambler when they first cross the line into *abnormal* gambling?

Presumably the first failure of the PFC and the subsequent inability to regulate one's gambling is precisely WHEN and HOW someone crosses the line from normal gambling into abnormal or problem gambling. And with each repeated failure the brain's *homeostasis* (balance point) changes to support the problem gambling, and the *Amygdala* begins to grow in order to cope with its new workload while the PFC is offline.

So it would most likely be erroneous to suggest that the PFC shutdown only affects Problem Gamblers. It could potentially ALL PLAYERS at some point whenever they gamble more than they intended or longer than they planned.]

There would also be questions about Company and Consumer law relating to the potentially negligent harming of customers. I am no expert, but think it possible that if a Company provides a product that can be shown to be harmful to some or potentially all of their customers, then the Company could most likely have to:

1. Display clear warnings at the point of sale about potential harm and associated risks (like the tobacco industry having to display a *'smoking kills'* warning on cigarette packets, along with pictures of cancerous lungs).

2. Refund anyone that hurts themselves using the product, immediately, in full, and without question.

It's beyond the remit of this book (and far from me to say) but I would imagine that it would be unacceptable in the 21st Century to cause an essential part of a **customer's brain to fail** in any way as a direct result of using a product? eg. as seen in the BBC Panorama documentary https://www.youtube.com/watch?v=BF5SzIN63w8

More so if there wasn't a suitable warning displayed prominently on the machine or screen along the lines of *"Gambling may affect a player's decision-making process resulting in irrational spending, impaired brain activity or other harmful consequences."*

And if the potential consequential loss of that brain failure resulted in **harm** in the form of financial wipe out, **loss of life** or **brain damage** then it could have far reaching implications for:

- The design of Electronic Gaming Machines (EGM's) with their auto-play and auto-repeat buttons which prompt gamblers to bet again almost instantly

- Gambling Laws and the ways in which they are enforced

- Gambling Advertising before the watershed (in sport and on TV etc) and online (social platforms etc)

- UK Consumer and Human Rights Laws

- Gambling Operators and the way in which they reimburse Problem Gamblers for lost funds (regardless of whether they self-excluded or not)
- Gambling being classified as a Mental Health issue

- The funding of Gambling Support programmes (currently only receiving one third that of drugs or alcohol support)

- Compensation being offered to the families of Gambling-Related Suicides covering damages and loss of future earnings

37673544R00204

Printed in Poland
by Amazon Fulfillment
Poland Sp. z o.o., Wrocław